D0898052

WELFARE, THE WORKING POOR, AND LABOR

WELFARE,

THE WORKING POOR,

AND LABOR

EDITED BY **LOUISE SIMMONS**

M.E.Sharpe
Armonk, New York
London, England

Library of Congress Cataloging-in-Publication Data

Welfare, the working poor, and labor / Louise Simmons, editor.
   p. cm.
Includes bibliographical references and index.
ISBN 0-7656-1300-X (alk. paper)
   1. Working poor—United States. 2. Working poor—Government policy—United States.
3. Labor policy—United States. 4. Public welfare—United States. I. Simmons, Louise B.,
1949–

HD8072.5.W45 2004
331.5—dc22   2003061799

Printed in the United States of America

The paper used in this publication meets the minimum requirements of
American National Standard for Information Sciences
Permanence of Paper for Printed Library Materials,
ANSI Z 39.48-1984.

BM (c) 10   9   8   7   6   5   4   3   2   1

In memory of my parents,
Frances and Louis Simmons,

and

dedicated to those who fight against great odds
for social and economic justice for the working poor

CONTENTS

Tables and Figures

Tables

Figures

Sources and Credits

Earlier versions of the following chapters appeared in the Winter 2002/ 2003 issue of *Working USA: The Journal of Labor and Society* 6, no. 3.

"Discipline and Seduction: The Campaign to Regulate American Workers" by Frances Fox Piven

"The Mirage of Welfare Reform" by Max B. Sawicky

"The Long Economic Downturn of the New Century" by Heather Boushey and Robert Cherry (earlier version titled "The Effect of the Economic Downturn on the Working Family")

"The Workforce Investment Act and the Labor Movement" by Helena Worthen

"Revolving Doors: Temp Agencies as Accelerators of Churning in Low-Wage Labor Markets" by Chirag Mehta and Nik Theodore (earlier version titled "Paying the Price for Flexibility: Unemployment Insurance and the Temporary Staffing Industry")

"Evaluating the Living Wage Strategy: Prospects, Problems, and Possibilities" by David J. Olson and Erich Steinman (earlier version by Margaret Levi, David Olson, and Erich Steinmen titled "Living-Wage Campaign and Laws")

"Labor-Welfare Linkages and the Imperative of Organizing Low-Wage Women Workers" by Louise Simmons

Max Sawicky's chapter is based on a paper titled "U.S. Welfare Reform: Learning Experience or Self-Delusion?" presented on July 27, 2002, at the conference "The Welfare State and Market Logic," at the University of Tokyo, Hongo Campus, sponsored by the Institute of Social Science, University of Tokyo.

James Jennings's chapter is based on a keynote address delivered at the University of Connecticut School of Social Work in West Hartford, Connecticut, on February 20, 2003, at a symposium "Revitalizing Our Cities/Confronting Urban Poverty," sponsored by the Urban and Community Studies Program at the University of Connecticut Tri-Campus, West Hartford Campus.

Acknowledgments

A volume like this is the product of many individuals' efforts. I am profoundly grateful to Manny Ness, the editor of *Working USA*, for encouraging me to take on this project and supporting the entire endeavor. I am deeply thankful to Myron Sharpe and Lynn Taylor of M.E. Sharpe, Inc., for their support, assistance, and patience. I also extend my gratitude to all of the authors whose work appears in the volume for the quality of their contributions and their cooperation in a complex process. I wish to acknowledge the assistance offered to me by the University of Connecticut School of Social Work, particularly by Dean Kay Davidson and Associate Dean Catherine Havens, who provided resources, and Taina Amaro, a promising graduate student, who helped in the manuscript preparation.

I want to recognize a number of individuals and organizations who have made it possible for my work on the connections between welfare and the labor movement to proceed. These include colleagues at the University of Connecticut and other institutions: Marcia Bok, Kenneth Neubeck, Mary Alice Neubeck, Nancy Churchill, and others who were involved in the Social Welfare Policy Study Group during the mid-1990s; colleagues in Community Organizing at the University of Connecticut; colleagues and friends from the United Association for Labor Education, Urban Affairs Association, and the Social Welfare Action Alliance who have shared information and exchanged ideas with me at various conferences; my treasured friends in the labor and progressive movements in Connecticut and elsewhere in the northeast who have encouraged this project, particularly Merrilee Milstein and Pearl Granat; my husband, Peter Chenette, his daughter, Emily, and my sister Wendy Simmons. I have the privilege of working with many incredibly devoted advocates, organizers, and grassroots leaders from an outstanding array of organizations and coalitions in Connecticut: the Connecticut Alliance for Basic Human Needs, the Connecticut Center for a New Economy, Citizens for Economic Opportunity, One-Connecticut, the Welfare Working Group, and all of the unions, organizations, and individuals who participate in these coalitions and our campaigns. These groups have counterparts nationally and in numerous states whose work parallels and contributes to all that we do in Connecticut. I also have the delight of working with many wonderful students at the University of Connecticut who participate in these organizations and struggles.

The job of editing a book in 2003 took place in the midst of very serious local, national, and international events: locally, an unprecedented state fiscal crisis and an all-out battle over what remnants of the social welfare state we could save in Connecticut; nationally and internationally, the disturbing events surrounding the invasion and occupation of Iraq. So, to all of the individuals and groups who organize, mobilize, and educate to keep our focus where it should be in these perilous times, immense gratitude. Finally, particularly to those young, struggling mothers who must wind their way through the maze of regulations, programs, eligibility determinations, late shifts, early mornings, and hard work, an affirmation of your worth and dignity.

Louise Simmons
Hartford, Connecticut

Introduction

Louise Simmons

Welfare reform as embodied in the Personal Responsibility and Work Opportunity Reconciliation Act of 1996 (PRWORA) signaled immense changes both in the lives of the poor and vulnerable in the United States and in the tone of policies and priorities that shape social programs. Given that PRWORA sets forth sixty-month lifetime limits for benefits and mandates that welfare recipients work in exchange for cash assistance, problems of welfare cannot be separated from problems of work, politics, organizing, and other questions of social and economic policy. Under the strictures of work requirements, the fate of poor women that was once in the domain of the Aid to Families with Dependent Children welfare program is now bound up with the realities of life in the low-wage workforce, and the issues associated with welfare are now inextricably woven into the problems of low-wage work.

The inauguration of the new welfare regime converged with several other important trends and events. First, welfare reform began implementation as the U.S. economy was recovering from a downturn and jobs were being created. Thus, many welfare recipients were able to find employment. The problem is whether or not these jobs necessarily lift them out of poverty. And they have new demands to balance between work and family, all the while on extremely low household budgets, even with employment. The labor market that welfare recipients are entering is one in which opportunities for low-wage workers to escape poverty are scarce and the single most important institution to protect workers, the labor movement, has been weakened after decades of assault from conservative political and corporate forces.

Welfare reform was also enacted at the same time as the labor movement in the United States was in the midst of change and a new leadership was taking the helm of the AFL-CIO. These changes, fomenting for years, heralded a new, more open exchange between academics and the labor movement. This exchange finds expression in many recent books and interesting new journals, in lively conferences, new or expanded programs for undergraduate, graduate, and nontraditional students, and a new role for scholar-activists who care about the future and the direction of the labor movement and working people in the United States and elsewhere. Moreover, with union density plummeting in recent decades, other critically important changes began to take place within the labor movement, including experimentation with new organizing strategies and the cultivation of progressive allies in other arenas of struggle.

Common concerns among labor, welfare activists, and the academics associated with these movements are the problem of poverty, the proliferation of low-wage work, and the fate of low-wage workers. Welfare rights activists are concerned about how many single parents will support their families as they enter this work environment. The labor movement, as it redefines its mission and confronts huge challenges to its own survival, must address the problems of the low-wage workforce that both represents potential new members but also can undercut the organized sectors. It must find the means of creating power for these workers and recapturing power for public sector work in this era.

A growing and interesting body of scholarship studies the impact of welfare reform. While this work capably assesses Temporary Assistance to Needy Families (TANF) program experiences and considers tensions of balancing family and work in the low-wage workforce, few analysts bring *labor* into the equation and address the inherent linkages among labor, welfare, and the low-wage work. In particular, a perspective that incorporates the experiences of the workers in welfare programs rarely surfaces. Thus, this volume hopefully fosters a necessary conversation among scholars and activists in these various worlds of the welfare system, the low-wage workforce, and the labor movement.

A number of the chapters are based on articles that appeared in the Winter 2002/2003 issue of *Working USA* and are updated or adapted for this book. Other chapters represent new original research and analysis by experts concerned with related themes. Several authors offer suggestions for action or for a reformulation of policy priorities that can alleviate the stress and tension that poor families are enduring in the post–welfare reform world. Together, they all contribute to the shaping of a common agenda for labor and welfare rights activists.

This book is organized into three sections. In the first section, the authors provide an analysis of the political forces that impacted the contours of welfare reform and the larger economic trends that confront welfare recipients and low-wage workers.

In Chapter 1, Frances Fox Piven argues that welfare reform is part of an aggressive class-based attack on the social welfare state with the objective of disciplining labor. Slicing through the arguments that center on the behavior and motivation of the poor offered by welfare reform's proponents, she illustrates where welfare reform fits within the larger corporate agenda for power and what is happening to women caught in the life transitions imposed by PRWORA.

In Chapter 2, Max Sawicky considers just how "successful" welfare reform has been and how to understand the patterns and trends that emerge from caseload declines and changes in the social safety net. He emphasizes that policy makers and the public have been overlooking the actual and potential harm to women and children in the welfare caseload.

Heather Boushey and Robert Cherry dissect patterns of employment and earnings, comparing the recent economic downturn to that of the early 1990s, in Chapter 3. They discuss the progress and setbacks of low-income women and people of color in the context of the economic downturn and analyze why this recent downturn is more deleterious than the earlier one to these groups of workers.

In Part II we discuss a number of issues arising in the programs that are supposed to serve the working poor. Also considered are problems for the labor movement and specific groups of workers in the context of welfare reform, changes in the employment and training system, and the increasingly privatized social welfare regime in the United States.

In Chapter 4, Fran Bernstein and Cecilia Perry, both policy analysts for the American Federation of State, County and Municipal Employees (AFSCME), depict the stress and tension of those on the front lines of the welfare state. They describe welfare reform from the point of view of caseworkers and eligibility workers in various states: the new demands, the conflicting mandates, the threat of privatization, and other problems of working in the new welfare regime. This is a particularly overlooked and underemphasized aspect of welfare reform: the voices of welfare workers need to be included in the story of welfare policy.

Manny Ness and Roland Zullo take up the question of privatization and how service workers in privatized settings are faring in Chapter 5. Their research involves in-depth interviews with union leaders in several settings in the New York metropolitan area. The living standards of service workers in public settings, particularly in the lesser-skilled segments of public sector service employment, are under constant threat from privatization, and this research highlights this facet of the new health and welfare system.

In Chapter 6, Helena Worthen considers the inherent challenges for the labor movement in the design of the Workforce Investment Act (WIA), the complex employment training program in the United States. She traces the history of previous job training programs and offers a critique of WIA in terms of its view of participants as isolated consumers rather than part of a class of workers with collective needs. She suggests how labor could play a more meaningful role in the WIA system.

Chirag Mehta and Nik Theodore investigate how the temporary staffing industry allows many employers to bypass the unemployment insurance (UI) system and shift the burden of the unemployment tax onto temporary agencies. With many welfare recipients finding work in the temp world, their ability to access the UI system in times of layoffs will be critical to their economic survival once they hit welfare time limits and no longer qualify for TANF. Thus, the ease with which employers can escape unemployment claims and shift them onto temporary agencies, and the ability of temp workers to claim UI, are critical questions for the very insecure low-wage workforce.

Section 3 offers some analysis of how various social forces are responding to welfare reform and the proliferation of low-wage work. Within this section, we consider the efficacy of the living-wage movement, how labor might incorporate welfare recipients into its organizing plans, and how to begin to reframe the manner in which we consider welfare reform into an agenda of human rights.

In Chapter 8, David Olson and Erich Steinman provide a thorough analysis of the living wage phenomenon. In over a hundred cities across the country, local governments, as well as other entities such as colleges, universities, and development districts, have enacted wage standards for firms with whom they do business. Olson and Steinman discuss the strengths and weaknesses of living-wage ordinances and also assess their possibilities for the creation of a social movement.

In Chapter 9, I take up the issues that specifically link labor and welfare and implore the labor movement to more thoroughly incorporate the needs of former welfare recipients as they enter the workforce. Unions can provide these new workers with a vehicle for a modicum of dignity, hope, and power in an otherwise often dismal job market.

To close this volume, James Jennings links the issues of welfare and urban poverty with the call for social justice in Chapter 10. He situates this call within a framework of human rights, a manner of recasting of questions of domestic poverty that is increasingly influencing progressive social thought. In an era of national focus on questions of security and on military conquest around the world, this human rights perspective can serve as a critical anchor in addressing domestic inequality.

This book is part of the beginning of the conversation. There is much more that can be said and entire future volumes to assemble. We can envision new research that deeply explores actual organizing experiences with former welfare recipients, evaluates how social welfare policies play out over the long term, assesses how low-wage workers survive the economic downturn of the early twenty-first century, and analyzes how the popular forces that organize around this set of issues can forcefully impact the national political agenda.

I

Working Poor and the
Contours of Welfare Reform

1

Discipline and Seduction

The Campaign to Regulate
American Workers

Frances Fox Piven

The Personal Responsibility and Work Opportunity Reconciliation Act of 1996—also known as "welfare reform"—was at least three decades in the making. The new welfare policy was enacted after a many-years-long campaign against existing welfare, or Aid to Families with Dependent Children (AFDC), by right-wing think tanks, politicians, and business organizations. The endlessly repeated arguments of the campaign asserted that Americans had been too generous, too kind. Generous AFDC benefits allowed women to opt out of wage labor and encouraged them in loose sexual behavior and out-of-wedlock births. The result was that AFDC in fact increased poverty, or at least it increased the underlying poverty that would exist in the absence of the program. The solution, as right-wing social critic Charles Murray famously recommended, was to eliminate welfare and thus force people who had become "dependent," addicted to the handout, to confront the discipline of the labor market. At first, the Murray solution appeared too drastic, too radical for incremental American politics. But as the campaign persisted, something close to Murray's recommendation has in fact been implemented.

The main thrust of the new regime, sometimes known as "work first," has been to make wage work the only option for poor mothers, no matter the smallness of their earnings, no matter the lack of reliable child care, no matter the crisis-ridden character of their lives. The operating administrative principle of "work first" is that cash assistance should be hard to get and hard to keep. Thus, federal law imposes a five-year lifetime limit on the receipt of assistance, and many states have imposed even more stringent limits. Federal law also requires the states to show that at least 50 percent of those on the welfare rolls are working at least thirty hours a week. President Bush now proposes to raise those requirements to 70 percent and forty hours. Even more important, although less obvious, the federal law gives the states—and the counties and private contractors to which the states devolve responsibility—wide latitude to sanction recipients with the loss of benefits if they transgress any of the system's myriad of new rules. And the states now also have the authority to rebuff, stall, or deny new applicants in a practice called "diversion." Moreover, since federal grants to the states are not reduced when caseloads and expenditures fall, the states have a strong incentive to sanction, divert, and deny.

The best-known consequence of the new regime, much heralded by politicians and the press, is that the welfare rolls have fallen precipitously, by more than half. We also know that of those who have left the rolls, perhaps 60 percent are working fairly steadily, at wages of about $7.50 an hour. Even with full-time work, which many welfare leavers do not have, this wage yields an income some $6 short of what the Economic Policy Institute estimates is necessary for a bare-bones budget. Moreover, many leavers are not working, or working only sporadically, and far less is known about their circumstances than about the welfare leaver "successes" who are working. Even the successes now confront new trouble. As unemployment rose during the recent economic slowdown, a good many of those employed former recipients found themselves jobless again. Because their work records were short and their earnings low, these women were unlikely to be eligible for unemployment benefits. And welfare, once the real unemployment insurance program for low-wage women workers, was effectively walled off from many of them as well.

To understand why this harsh regime has become the policy of the nation, we need to look beyond welfare itself, and beyond welfare policy discussions, to a range of related changes that have occurred in domestic policy over the past three decades. Taken one by one, each policy change may seem credibly explained by particular policy discourses. But taken together, the changes suggest something larger at work. I think welfare cutbacks can best be understood as part of a multifaceted campaign oriented to intensifying labor market discipline, especially in the lower reaches of the workforce. To be sure, the political talk that justifies these policies is about other things, about restoring civil order, for example, or shoring up two-parent families, or giving workers a stake in the American dream. But so was the talk that justified the very similar campaign of the late nineteenth century about other things. Outdoor relief was eliminated or rolled back; people called tramps or hobos were rounded up, presumably to restore order, civility, and morality to American life. In both periods, the talk itself was politics, a politics to make a campaign to discipline working people palatable, even to working people themselves.

So I turn to the elements of the larger campaign which I think make welfare reform comprehensible. They include a three-decades-long assault on unions, in the workplace and in politics. Unions have many flaws, of course, but overall they do raise wages and help workers secure some rights in the workplace. Since the early 1970s, big business has been determined to weaken unions for just those reasons. This stance first became evident with the growing intransigence of management in contract negotiations, where, for example, they began to insist on two-tier contracts with sharply lower wages and benefits for new employees, an arrangement that was insidious in its effects on union solidarity. The highlight of this stage of the antiunion war was the standoff between President Reagan and the air controllers union, which resulted in mass layoffs of the striking workers. Since then, although less visibly, business has continued to lobby successfully for the rule changes and probusiness appointments that have made the National Labor Relations Board, which oversees collective bargaining rights, virtually toothless. The result is that union density has plummeted to pre-1930s levels.

Or consider contemporary new-style, top-down educational reform proposals. As usual, the rhetoric is about educational excellence. But the emphasis on standards and testing, on rote teaching methods, on phonics and classroom discipline, suggests something more like the dumbing down of public education. So does the cast of characters who are the main educational reformers, including the Business Roundtable and the testing companies. The push for privatization, another aspect of contemporary educational reform, has the added payoff of making public education a new field for profiteering, just as the privatization in many places of the administration of welfare has made it a field for profiteering.

And then there is the growing trend to privatize pensions. As with the privatization of schools, prisons, and welfare, the persistence with which backers of privatization of Social Security have pressed their cause reflects in part the profits that Wall Street will earn from these investments. But there is more to privatization than that. The rise of 401(k)s is illustrative. Employment-based social benefits, mainly in the form of pensions and health care plans that depend on employers, have always been suspect for the simple reason that they are another way to tie workers who always face the risk of illness and the prospect of old age to the firm that employs them, no matter the other conditions of employment. Labor historian Nelson Lichtenstein (1989) once said that these programs should be understood as a form of serfdom (see also Lichtenstein 2002). The increased reliance on 401(k)s underscores Lichtenstein's point. Business lobbyists press to retain employee stock options and other forms of employee investments in the companies that employ them, even in the wake of the Enron pension debacle, because, these lobbyists argue, these arrangements produce more worker loyalty and commitment. Enron workers lost 1.3 billion of the 2 billion pension dollars they had invested in the company, and so did other workers' pensions take big hits as a result of mutual fund investments in Enron stock.

As private pension programs expanded, the public income support programs initiated in the 1930s and enlarged in the 1960s have been rolled back. Cuts in cash assistance under welfare are an aspect of this decrease, but these cuts are dwarfed by the changes that have occurred in Social Security, unemployment insurance, food stamps, and Medicaid. The great achievement of these programs taken together was that they made working people more secure in the face of the exigencies of old age or unemployment or illness or disability. Unemployed people who knew they could get benefits were less terrified, less likely to take any job offered on any terms. In the recession of the mid-1970s, more than two-thirds of the unemployed received these benefits. In other words, the most vulnerable people were at least partially shielded from market sanctions.

In the 1990s, about one-third of the unemployed received benefits, largely because of arcane changes in the formulas determining eligibility. Or consider Old Age Survivors and Dependents Insurance, the program we call Social Security. When the program was inaugurated in 1935, the talk was about removing old people from a crowded labor market where they did not fare well and where they undermined the bargaining power of younger workers. Now, with little fanfare, the age of Social Security eligibility has been raised to sixty-seven years, albeit gently by one month a year so as not to provoke an outcry, and earnings by the old are treated more generously in calculating Social Security benefit levels so as to encourage retirees to take the jobs that fast food restaurants, for example, offer. And not only has eligibility for food stamps been tightened, but because the administration of both the food stamp and Medicaid programs were always tied to welfare, welfare cutbacks have also resulted in a marked decline in the percentage of eligible people who actually receive these other benefits.

And then there are the cutbacks in cash income support associated with welfare reform. Quite apart from the impact on family and community well-being, between 2.5 and 3 million women have been pushed into the labor market, some to get jobs, others to hunt for them. These numbers are significant. Millions of desperate women who otherwise would have been raising their children with welfare grants are working or scrambling for work. This is roughly equivalent to a two to three percentage point increase in the unemployment rate in its impact on worker bargaining power and, of course, it affects the bargaining power of lower-wage workers most directly. There are also cultural dimensions to welfare reform as a strategy for intensifying worker discipline, but before I turn to them I want to say a little about the wider cultural campaign to celebrate markets and reinforce labor market discipline.

It hardly needs to be demonstrated that American politics has been overtaken by the celebration of markets associated with neoliberalism. One might view it as a renaissance of nineteenth-century laissez-faire and its depiction of markets as operating according to something akin to natural law. This time, however, the deifying of markets gains credibility from the globalization of market exchange, which seems to make merely national governments helpless to intervene, except by putting domestic investment and trade at risk. This is not the occasion to scrutinize this view carefully, and I will have to be content with asserting that it is wildly exaggerated, especially when it is applied to the United States, since our domestic economy is huge and our government has great economic and political power in setting the rules of the international economy. My point now is simply that this argument, pushed to extremes by ideological fanatics, undermines the democratic capacity of working people to press government for protective measures.

Moreover, neoliberalism or neolaissez-faire has been shored up by a campaign to depict Wall Street as a game in which everyone can play and everyone can win. This is part of the meaning of the expansion of 401(k)s. Hoodwinked workers whose pensions are invested in the stock market tie their hopes for a better life to the Dow Jones average. This investment and this illusion allays workers' resentments about lagging wages and shrinking public benefits. It turns them away from the old struggles for better wages, better workplace conditions, and better public programs, as they watch the roulette wheel whirl in the vain hope that it will stop at their number.

Welfare reform is part of this cultural transformation. Consider the impact of the campaign against welfare on public opinion, as women on welfare were decried on all sides as dependent, meaning they were addicted to the dole, guilty of sexual excess and license, the contemporary inheritors of nineteenth-century style moral iniquity. The new welfare regimen itself underlines this form of cultural teaching by stripping recipients of rights and forcing them to endure demeaning bureaucratic rituals. If farmers who received federal crop subsidies were subject to the same invasive investigations as welfare recipients, the public understanding of the status of farmers and the meaning of the subsidies would also gradually shift. In 1986, Mickey Kaus, a conservative critic of the old AFDC program, made explicit the purpose of a degrading welfare system when he said that the reason to put Betsy Smith to work sweeping streets and cleaning buildings—which is exactly what some workfare programs now require—was not only to deter Betsy Smith from having an illegitimate child but so that the "sight of Betsy Smith sweeping streets after having her illegitimate child will discourage her younger sisters and neighbors from doing as she did" (Kaus 1986). And, much as Kaus predicted, these new welfare rituals are having an impact on poor women. More important, they have an impact on all low-wage workers as welfare becomes more demeaning and as work, even low-wage and disrespected work, by contrast gains value.

So who is doing this campaign? And why? I think the effort to intensify worker discipline dates from the early 1970s, when corporate America was grappling with narrowing profit margins. The squeeze on profits resulted partly from intensifying competition from Japan and West Germany—only recall how the auto industry was thrown into disarray by the arrival of small, efficient cars on American markets—and partly from rising prices for raw materials, especially rising oil prices. The squeeze also resulted, however, from rising wages and growing expenditures on income support programs that undergirded wages. And business costs had also grown because of the expansion of workplace and environmental regulation. All these latter costs reflected the gains made by the protest movements of the 1960s and the turbulence and electoral upsets they set in motion. No wonder the Great Society has become an epithet in the mouths of conservative critics.

The corporations' response to these developments was to try to recover their competitive edge, to enlarge profits, by lowering wages and social benefits, by pushing back regulation, and by slashing business taxes. To accomplish this, American business leaders who had grown fat and lazy during the twenty-five years after World War II, when America's economic preeminence was unchallenged, mobilized to do politics. They formed new peak business organizations and revived old business organizations like the National Association of Manufacturers and the Chamber of Commerce, organizations that had virtually become dormant during the heady postwar years of business success. CEOs retooled themselves and became lobbyists, vice presidents for "public affairs" were created, and business became a major Washington presence, as a flourishing K Street demonstrates. Lastly, business money flowed to politicians and their campaigns, to buy access and influence.

In the area of social policy, however, business groups acted out their politics cautiously. In effect, they employed front men, the right-wing think tanks funded by business but presenting themselves as class-neutral, intellectual arbiters of policy. The names are familiar: Heritage, Cato, the Hudson Institute, the American Enterprise Institute, the Manhattan Institute. The think tanks became the mouthpieces of a business class mobilized to do battle with the social policies inherited from the New Deal and the Great Society. They sponsored public intellectuals like George Gilder and Charles Murray, they wrote and published books, they deluged congressional offices with daily reports giving their take on policies, they promoted their spokespeople on TV talk shows, they flooded the newspapers with op eds. And their agenda was the business agenda of dismantling the social protections painfully developed during the twentieth century. In significant measure, that agenda has succeeded.

What then can be done to restore the public policies that brought a measure of security to the lives of working and poor Americans? Some hints at an answer are gained, I think, by sober scrutiny of periods of egalitarian reform in American history. The 1930s gave us federal protection of labor rights, and the first national social welfare programs, including AFDC. The 1960s expanded those programs, and improved them too, bringing something like the rule of law to the administration of AFDC, for example. In both these periods, the poor and their advocates mobilized in protest, raised new demands, made trouble, enough trouble to penetrate electoral politics and threaten dominant electoral coalitions. If we look even further back into the nineteenth century, we can see a similar pattern in the success of the abolitionists. The abolitionists were despised and harassed for the issues they raised and the trouble they made, but their issues and their trouble broke up the intersectional national parties and created the conditions that led to civil war and emancipation.

What about now? Before 9/11 and the ensuing war on terror and then on Iraq, there were clear signs that widening inequality in the United States together with corporate abuse of democratic politics was nourishing a new wave of protests. We could see it in the dramatic anticorporate globalization demonstrations, in antisweatshop campaigns on campuses, in the resurgence of the labor movement, in living wage campaigns in the cities. Those protests have been muffled by the triumphalism of war making, which, whatever else it is, has also become a mask, a charade to shield from view the public policies that made the rich richer and the poor poorer, within the United States and abroad. The vice president has said that the war on terror may take fifty years. But it is unlikely to succeed as a shield and diversion from the policies that encourage business greed and enforce labor discipline for fifty years. It may not even work for one election cycle. People do regain their footing, and voices of dissent are important in helping to make that happen.

References

Kaus, Mickey. 1986. "The Work Ethic State." *New Republic*, 7 July: 22–32.
Lichtenstein, Nelson. 1989. "From Corporatism to Collective Bargaining: Organized Labor and the Eclipse of Social Democracy in the Postwar Era." In *The Rise and Fall of the New Deal Order, 1930–1980*, ed. Steve Freaser and Gary Gerstle, pp. 140–45. Princeton, NJ: Princeton University Press.
Lichtenstein, Nelson. 2002. *State of the Union: A Century of American Labor.* Princeton, NJ: Princeton University Press.

2

The Mirage of Welfare Reform

Max B. Sawicky

> I think it's fair to say the debate is over. We now know that
> welfare reform works.
> —*President Bill Clinton, 1997*

> While family income since passage of the welfare reform
> bill in 1996 generally improved, outcomes for independent
> single-parent families are alarming.
> —*Sheila Zedlewski, Urban Institute, 2002*

In 1996 the U.S. Congress passed the Personal Responsibility and Work
Opportunity Reconciliation Act (PRWORA), providing that a new program
called Temporary Assistance for Needy Families (TANF) would
replace Aid to Families with Dependent Children (AFDC). Not long
after the inauguration of TANF, the program was widely hailed as a
brilliant success. Today it continues to enjoy nearly universal approbation.
But evidence for the program's success is less certain than commonly
thought. We are told that under TANF, welfare recipients are
securing employment and enjoying a higher standard of living, but reasons
for skepticism abound.

As might be expected, PRWORA legislation was not the only important
development of the 1990s in antipoverty policy. Good news attributed
to welfare reform could be due to other factors:

- *The record performance of the U.S. labor market* in the late 1990s.
  Between 1997 and 2001, the unemployment rate was usually below
  5 percent. Wage growth attributable to tight labor markets also

reached the lowest-paid workers, particularly women and minorities (Bernstein and Baker 2002).

- *The earned income tax credit (EITC) was significantly expanded* in 1993, providing a wage subsidy of 34 or 40 percent for a worker with one or two children, respectively. Today the EITC can provide as much as $4,000 annually to a family with two or more children. The latest research on the EITC finds positive effects on work effort (Ellwood 2000; Meyer and Rosenbaum 2000).
- *The minimum wage was raised* between 1995 and 1997 from $4.25 to $5.15. Recent research on the minimum wage has found that it reduces poverty and raises employment, contrary to the claims of its critics (Card and Krueger 1995).
- *What has been called the "work support system" was expanded* by a factor of eight since the mid-1980s (Congressional Budget Office 1998, cited in Sawhill and Haskins 2002). Along with the EITC and minimum wage, this set of programs includes a child tax credit of $400 per child, state government–financed earned income credits, the State Children's Health Insurance Program, and child care subsidies. All of these programs are targeted at low-income families with employed adults. Cuts in supplemental security income and food stamps in 1996, on both of which many of the poor depend, were partially restored between 1997 and 1999.
- *The social insurance tax (payroll tax) burden on the lowest income quintile rose from 1979 to 1989*, then remained constant (Congressional Budget Office 1998). The combined rate on employer and employee went up over three percentage points to a total of 15.3 between 1980 and 1990. The effect could have been to reduce low-wage jobs and inflate the welfare caseload, thereby facilitating subsequent reductions due to expansion of the EITC.

Seldom has the United States enjoyed such fair weather for the launch of a new welfare reform. We should have expected better outcomes regardless of what sort of reform had been attempted or even if no reform at all had been tried.

Data pertaining to the impact of welfare reform originates from a variety of sources. This chapter focuses on *trends in the populations at risk of poverty.* Invariably the popular discussion of success is limited to the decline in the caseload and findings of employment of former welfare recipients. Under the premise that any welfare program or antipoverty strategy ought to be assessed in terms of its impact on *potential* participants, as well as actual ones, we could consider the changing characteristics of those who are most likely to come into contact with the welfare system, those who fall near or below the poverty line.

The disadvantage of this data is that it may not be easy to relate changes in groups to changes in one or more programs affecting a subset of persons in that group. Another problem is that this data lacks a counterfactual; a change is not easy to compare to what might have happened under alternative policies.

Nothing Succeeds Like Success

The degree of consensus on welfare reform is reflected in the statement of a group of eminent, moderate, and objective U.S. scholars: "The welfare rolls have declined greatly, more mothers than ever are working, the average income of female-headed families—especially those who are never married—is increasing, and poverty has dropped substantially" (Haskins, Sawhill, and Weaver 2001, 8).

Our discussion will show the possibilities for different summary characterizations of the fruits of U.S. welfare reform.

Aggregate data can mislead in many ways. Correlations can be spurious. Important factors may go unnoticed or may be difficult to measure. Observed trends, even accurately observed, can reflect very little information. Causation can be reversed or two-way.

Such issues notwithstanding, the trend data are exactly the sort of information that animate commentators and politicians. These channels of opinion dominate the public debate and its political currents. In the final analysis it is the condition of the population that is of greatest interest.

The Timeline of Relevant Policy Changes

In evaluating trends in aggregate data, some key dates should be kept in mind:

> *1981:* Passage of the Omnibus Budget Reconciliation Act, based in large part on the first proposed budget of the Reagan administration, entailed significant contraction of the "thirty and a third" rule in AFDC. This rule provided for an "earnings disregard" in calculating benefits. The idea was that if income was below a

certain standard, one-third of each additional dollar earned would be disregarded in determining the benefit that resulted by subtracting income from the standard level. In effect these disregards constituted negative income taxes, albeit ones that were subject to many conditions. The upshot is that the implicit marginal tax rate on labor for those in the AFDC program was raised from 67 percent to 100 percent—a dollar of additional earnings meant a dollar less of cash assistance. Considering payroll taxes and benefit cutoffs in other programs, the welfare recipient's marginal tax rate could easily exceed 100 percent.

1983: In response to the recommendations of a special commission that anticipated future problems in Social Security, Congress increased the payroll (social insurance) tax by three percentage points, to 15.3 percent.

1988: The Family Support Act was passed, greatly expanding the scope for waivers in AFDC. Also passed was the JOBS program, providing a modest amount of funds targeted at work preparation and job training for welfare recipients.

1993: As part of the first budget proposal of the Clinton administration, the earned income tax credit was significantly expanded. Clinton also began to accelerate the pace of granting waivers.

1996: PRWORA was enacted.

1997: National implementation of PRWORA began. Congress created a new Welfare to Work Program, a new child tax credit, and a new State Children's Health Insurance Program (SCHIP).

TANF universalized departures, known as "waivers," from the AFDC program that had been sponsored for the previous decade. It is reasonable, on this account and broadly speaking, to mark the U.S. business cycle from 1990 to 2001 as the gestation period for U.S. welfare reform. Given the incremental accretion of waivers, leading to passage of PRWORA, followed by a gradual buildup of national implementation, we might expect a similar pattern of effects: gradual growth and an acceleration after 1997. Note that "results" need not be limited to desirable outcomes.

The evolution of welfare before PRWORA is evidently not too clear. Nathan and Gais (2001) claim that the more important waivers were not implemented until after 1995, while Haskins, Sawhill, and Weaver (2001) say that "over half the states were implementing their own welfare reform programs under waivers by 1994." Since PRWORA was not passed until 1996, we would not see implementation begin until 1997, and many of the effects of that implementation might not be observed until 1998 or later.

The Trends

Caseloads

Caseload reduction is invariably highlighted as the signal achievement of welfare reform. This is at least a little curious because a simple act of administrative fiat—outright, immediate abolition of AFDC—would have accomplished 100 percent caseload reduction instantly. For caseload reduction to be an achievement, the logical implication is that some other developments accompanied it. We will return to this issue.

In the 1990s, the caseload of AFDC/TANF declined from over 5 million families to 2.2 million. No single trend is cited more often as a sign of welfare reform's success. This net drop entails a rise from 1990 to 1994, then a decline for every succeeding year.

By this simple metric no effect of waivers on the caseload is visible before 1995, consistent with the finding of Nathan and Gais (2001), but not with that of Haskins, Sawhill, and Weaver (2001). The latter part of the decade happens to coincide with a period of historic lows in U.S. unemployment, when the bulk of the caseload reduction also transpired.

One potentially misleading aspect of the caseload data lies in the fact that these data do not include families unless they receive cash assistance (Fremstad and Neuberger 2002). The caseload reductions are the "cash caseload." Over a million families could be uncounted for this reason.

Assorted services designed at facilitating labor market participation, such as child care or job training, are financed under TANF, and presumably some persons would have difficulty functioning without such help. So the caseload decline is not necessarily coincident with a decline in dependency, unless we narrow the definition to entail the receipt of cash assistance. This means that a family that needed medical services, transportation aid, an earned income tax credit, and child care to function would not be classified as "dependent" by the cash caseload metric.

States have established diversion programs that move applicants for

TANF benefits into other programs. In this respect as well, TANF caseload data fail to account for the use of public benefits from other programs by those who might otherwise be enrolled in TANF.

Female Unemployment

Regarding the unemployment rate for women, only 5 percent of TANF families have two adult recipients. Two-thirds have one recipient, and the remainder—29 percent—are child-only cases. Eighty-nine percent of adults in TANF are heads of their households (DHHS 2000), which means that most households consist of children with a single resident parent. We could speculate that labor demand pulled women off the welfare rolls, and reform had no effect, or that reform increased the supply of labor offered by women.

The unemployment decline begins before the caseload reduction by several years. As we will see, positive developments such as this in a number of social indicators precede the implementation of TANF in 1997, the passage of TANF legislation in 1996, and even the beginning of the caseload decline in 1995. Whether the accretion of waivers before 1996 should get the credit is an open question.

It happens that the number of cases and unemployed women are comparable, although they are not identical groups. In 1991 and 1992, it is possible that the caseload was directly expanded by changes in unemployment. But in 1993 and 1994 the changes are in the opposite direction—caseloads up, unemployment down. After 1994, it appears that the caseload reductions vastly exceed reductions in female unemployment, in the range of 200,000 to 400,000 families. This presents a different question. Maybe the labor market is responsible for part of the caseload reduction. But if reform caused reductions that moved women into jobs, what was the fate of the remaining families?

The number of female-headed households in poverty does indeed decrease for most years after 1993, but by not nearly as much as the caseload decline. As before, we have to wonder what happened to the excess of caseload decline relative to the decline in the number of families headed by women. Elsewhere we note the lack of change in the number of single-mother families throughout the 1990s, after a period of growth from 1989 to 1993.

Female unemployment fell after 1992. If there was some shift in the composition of employment toward women with children, and away from women without children, the caseload reductions could have been absorbed by the overall growth of the labor market.

Labor market data should be distinguished from what is reported as work or employment by welfare systems themselves. PRWORA includes mandates on states to achieve certain levels of participation in "work activities." When states meet these mandates, public officials issue press releases reporting the good news.

Employment of Mothers

Another relevant trend is in the employment history of mothers. Single mothers' employment underwent a significant upward trend in the 1990s, but it began in 1992, before the start of the caseload decline and the new legislation, and before most waivers. The percentages in question are that 57 percent of single mothers were employed at some point during the year in 1992, and 71 percent in 1999 (Congressional Research Service cited in *Green Book 2000*). Never-married mothers worked more too, but this trend had been rising since 1986 and began accelerating in 1992. In terms of single mothers, the best that could be said for the process of waivers leading to reform is that at most 14 percent of single mothers were induced to work. Offsetting this impact is the extent to which the record-setting labor market of the latter 1990s was the cause.

Children of Unmarried Mothers

The preeminent archetype invoked by welfare critics is the teenage, unmarried mother. Between 1980 and 1993, the rate of births per 1,000 unmarried women, ages fifteen to nineteen, increased significantly, from 87.9 to 102.4. From 1993 to 1998, it decreased to below the 1980 level, to 83.4. This trend fits reasonably well with claims for PRWORA. For women aged twenty to twenty-four, and twenty-five to twenty-nine, however, decreases after 1993 end in two years, after which both rates increase again. In terms of the buildup of TANF, this is exactly backward. The percentage of children not living with either parent is down only slightly from 1995 to 1998. By way of background, the fertility rate for all women trended down after 1990 (*Green Book 2000*).

Haskins, Sawhill, and Weaver (2001) point out that any improvement in a social indicator such as this one could itself be the cause of improvements in areas like employment or income. The likely reality is a tangle of factors in which each works on the others, making program evaluation difficult.

Two-Parent Families

In theory, a source of dependency is the failure to maintain two-parent families. The trend in families headed by mothers was up from 1989 to 1993 by about 18 percent, then more or less constant at about 9.9 million from 1993 to 1998. In this case, the positive development is well in advance of most waivers and welfare reform, and the lack of further progress raises a question about the effectiveness of welfare reform in this vein. Of course, it is always possible to argue that one-parent families would have increased without welfare reform!

Income and Poverty

For all groups in the population, the poverty rate in the 1990s shows decreases. The declines all begin well before the passage of PRWORA. Depending on the group in question, there is sometimes more of a decrease before 1997 than after. Both of these suggest factors other than TANF in operation, though they do not exclude TANF as a contributing factor. For instance, for the group least likely to be affected by welfare reform—white non-Hispanic married-couple families—the peak year of poverty in the 1990s is 1993, with a rate of 4.7 percent. This falls to 3.5 by 1997, the year of TANF implementation, and thereafter falls by only 0.2 percentage points more, to 3.3 percent (*Green Book 2000*).

Regarding trends for groups more at risk of poverty, specifically families with children less than eighteen years of age: Keeping in the mind the plunge in the caseload after 1994, the ideal reflection in terms of TANF effects would be some kind of similar drop in poverty.

In all cases but blacks, some of the reductions lag the caseload drop and incidentally coincide with the record lows in U.S. unemployment. Some reductions predate the caseload drop.

Alternative measures of poverty for single mothers raise similar problems of interpretation, typically showing poverty reductions that begin after 1993, before the caseload reductions, before most waivers, and well before the passage of PWRORA (*Green Book 2000*).

The overall reduction in the number of families in poverty after 1993 is 1.8 million, most of whom (1.7 million) had children. A closer match to the TANF clientele, however, would be families with children but lacking a married couple. The decrease in the number of families in poverty for this group was 1.1 million. We remind the reader that the caseload drop is well over 2 million, so a high proportion of those who left TANF could not have escaped poverty, particularly before 2000.

The 1990s drop in poverty should be put in a longer historical perspective. The recent low point in the poverty rate, typically viewed as the victory of welfare reform over the dysfunctional AFDC program, was 11.3 percent in 2000. (The rate went up to 11.7 the following year.) But in 1979 the rate was 11.7 percent, by the same reasoning the fruits of the aforementioned AFDC. In earlier years it was lower still. So should we say that welfare reform reduced poverty by less than 1 percent?

Diversity and "Deep Poverty"

The poverty population is diverse and fluid. We cannot expect it to react uniformly to any development or program innovation. One consideration is what story might lie beneath average changes, the poverty rate, and other summary measures. An average increase could mask a combination of increases for some and decreases for others. The poverty rate fails to reflect any decreases in income for those already below the poverty line, or increases for those already above it. Both of these developments appear to have taken place in the 1990s.

For all parties concerned, the most important datum is the earnings of those who leave welfare. Haskins, Sawhill, and Weaver (2001) report that, considering the bottom income quintile of mother-headed families, earnings increased between 1993 and 1999 by a huge 82 percent. This quintile includes most single-parent families (as opposed to two-parent or no-parent cases) who enter and leave the TANF program. In 1998, it consisted of 1.3 million families.

The annual earnings levels in question are extremely low. The percent growth refers to a level of $1,331 in 1993 and $2,417 in 1999. At an hourly wage of $7, not untypical for a TANF leaver, the implied "value-added" over the period amounts to less than two additional days' work per month. Earnings in the bottom income quintile of single mothers increased by $390 annually (Loprest 2002).

Wendell Primus (1999) found that the bottom income quintile of single-mother families had increased incomes from 1993 to 1995, but either decreases (for the bottom decile) or no increase (for the second decile) for the following years. Haskins, Sawhill, and Weaver (2001) find that the earnings gains were more than offset by cuts in cash benefits and food stamps; the program that made it possible for this group to come out ahead was the EITC. Haskins and Primus (2000) note that disposable income (income after taxes, but including the EITC) for the bottom income quintile of single-mother families fell by 4 percent between 1995 and 1998. Zedlewski (2002) finds a real income loss of 8 percent for the bottom quintile of single mothers living independently between 1996 and 1998. She also finds an increase in the number of families whose incomes fell below 50 percent of the poverty line. Loprest (2002) finds an increase in "extreme poverty" from 1996 to 1998 for single mothers living independently, and no decrease for all families with children.

Potentially compounding a loss in income is the decline in the number of families with children enrolled in Medicaid (down two percentage points) and food stamps (down eight percentage points) (Zedlewski 2002).

Developments in the bottom quintile of single-mother families would be a bit less worrisome if the number of such families was reduced. From 1996 to 1998, the percent reduction was 8 percent (Zedlewski 2002).

Unemployment rates for 1995 to 1997 compared very well with prior historical experience, and the best was yet to come. But Sawhill (2001) reports, "Overall, 700,000 families were significantly worse off in 1999 than their counterparts in 1995."

How welfare reform should be judged in this light is open to debate. On one hand, we could hypothesize that without the encouragement of work, the work-conditioned benefits would not have been available, so PRWORA really did provide income gains for some people. On the other hand, it is possible that a focus on wage subsidies such as an expanded EITC (Cherry and Sawicky 2000; Sawicky and Cherry 2001; Sawicky, Cherry, and Denk 2002) would have provided greater returns than the increases in TANF resources per beneficiary, plus investments in the complex administrative machinery of the new state welfare systems.

Another way of going further beneath the surface of summary measures can be found in the "hardship" literature. The National Survey of American Families provides data on the extent to which families experience such adversities as food insecurity, inadequate housing, inadequate child care, and inadequate health care. Boushey (2002) found that families who left TANF in 1999 fared worse in these dimensions than those who left in 1995, although economic conditions and a more advanced stage of welfare reform should have yielded opposite results. In general, at least a third of those surveyed experienced some kind of hardship, including those who left TANF and were working full-time.

A common axiom in U.S. social policy is "first, do no harm." The possibility that welfare reform could have benefited some but harmed others raises the problem of evaluating the implied trade-off. While the public might be reconciled to a lower standard of living for some under a new work-based welfare system, it is not clear that they would accept the implications of outcomes characterized as "significantly worse off" or "alarming" for the dependent children most affected.

Conclusion

Two primary implications can be drawn from this discussion. First, reported income gains, reductions in poverty rates, and improvements in other social indicators abstract in a misleading way from the time profile of such changes, which often predates most welfare reform and does not move consistently with the evolution of reform.

Second, the fates of single-mother families, leavers, those expelled from TANF because of sanctions, and those who have escaped the monitoring capacities of state governments are substantially underemphasized in the public debate and even in policy reviews by competent scholars. The "first, do no harm" axiom has been grossly violated. The fate of children in families subject to sanction, and those who have otherwise left TANF permanently, must be ascertained, with respect to family income, nutrition, health, domestic violence, child abuse, and school performance.

By the aggregate data, U.S. welfare reform's achievements are uncertain and ambiguous, and its harm to a significant minority of poor families is manifest. Contrary to the complacency of a wide assortment of politicians, the debate over welfare reform is not over. It is just beginning.

References

Bernstein, Jared, and Dean Baker. 2002. "Full Employment: Don't Give It Up Without a Fight." Working Paper No. 122. Washington, DC: Economic Policy Institute.

Boushey, Heather. 2002. "Former Welfare Families Need More Help: Hardships Await Those Making Transition to Workforce." Briefing paper. Washington, DC: Economic Policy Institute.

Card, David, and Alan B. Krueger. 1995. *Myth and Measurement: The New Economics of the Minimum Wage.* Princeton, NJ: Princeton University Press.

Cherry, Robert, and Max B. Sawicky. 2000. "Giving Tax Credit Where Credit Is Due: A Universal Unified Child Credit That Expands the EITC and Cuts Taxes for Working Families." Briefing paper. Washington, DC: Economic Policy Institute.

Congressional Budget Office. 1998. *Policy Changes Affecting Mandatory Spending for Low-Income Families Not Receiving Cash Welfare.* Washington, DC.

Ellwood, David T. 2000. "The Impact of the Earned Income Tax Credit and Social Policy Reforms on Work, Marriage, and Living Arrangements." *National Tax Journal* 53, no. 4, part 2 (December): 1063–1106.

Fremstad, Shawn, and Zoe Neuberger. 2002. "TANF's 'Uncounted' Cases: More than One Million Working Families Receiving TANF-Funded Services Not Counted in TANF Caseload." Washington, DC: Center on Budget and Policy Priorities.

The Green Book: Background Material and Data on Programs Within the Jurisdiction of the Committee on Ways and Means. Various editions. Washington, DC: U.S. Government Printing Office.

Haskins, Ron, and Wendell Primus. 2000. "Point-Counterpoint: Perspectives on Welfare Reform and Children." *JCPR Newsletter*, 11 August.

Haskins, Ron, Isabel Sawhill, and Kent Weaver. 2001. *Welfare Reform: An Overview of Effects to Date.* Policy Brief No. 1. Washington, DC: Brookings Institution.

Loprest, Pamela J. 2002. "Making the Transition from Welfare to Work: Successes but Continuing Concerns." In *Welfare Reform: The Next Act,* ed. Alan Weil and Kenneth Finegold, pp. 17–32. Washington, DC: Urban Institute, 2002.

Meyer, Bruce D., and Dan T. Rosenbaum. 2000. "Making Single Mothers Work: Recent Tax and Welfare Policy and Its Effects." *National Tax Journal* 53, no. 4, part 2 (December): 1027–63.

Nathan, Richard P., and Thomas L. Gais. 2001. "Is Devolution Working?" *Brookings Review* 19, no. 3 (Summer): 25–29.

Primus, Wendell. 1999. *National Problems, Local Solutions: Federalism at Work. Part III. Welfare Reform Is Working: A Report on State and Local Initiatives.* Hearing before the Committee on Government Reform and Oversight, U.S. House of Representatives, 106th Cong. 1st sess., April 22. Available at www.house.gov/reform.

Sawhill, Isabel. 2001. "From Welfare to Work." *Brookings Review* 19, no. 3 (Summer): 4–7.

Sawhill, Isabel, and Ron Haskins. 2002. "Welfare Reform and the Work Support System." *Welfare Reform and Beyond.* Policy Brief No. 17. Washington DC: Brookings Institution.

Sawicky, Max B. 1999. *The End of Welfare? Consequences of Federal Devolution for the Nation.* Armonk, NY: M.E. Sharpe.

Sawicky, Max B., and Robert Cherry. 2001. "Making Work Pay with Tax Reform." Issue brief. Washington, DC: Economic Policy Institute.

Sawicky, Max B., Robert Cherry, and Robert Denk. 2002. "The Next Tax Reform:

Advancing Tax Benefits for Children." Working paper. Washington, DC: Economic Policy Institute.

U.S. Department of Health and Human Services, Administration for Children and Families, Office of Planning, Research, and Evaluation (DHHS). 2000. *Temporary Assistance for Needy Families Program: Third Annual Report to Congress.* Available at www.acf.dhhs.gov/programs/opre/director.htm.

Zedlewski, Sheila R. 2002. "Family Incomes: Rising, Falling, or Holding Steady?" In *Welfare Reform: The Next Act*, ed. Alan Weil and Kenneth Finegold, pp. 53–78. Washington, DC: Urban Institute.

3

The Long Economic Downturn of the New Century

Heather Boushey and Robert Cherry

The recovery of the early 2000s marks the longest period of sustained employment decline in the post–World War II period. Unfortunately, at this writing in the fall of 2003, there are few signs of unemployment going back down anytime soon. Current economic policies at the federal level and the fiscal crisis in the states are not helping the situation. As in recessions generally, workers at the bottom end of the income spectrum have been hit the hardest. What happens to workers at the bottom is, however, not the focus of media or policy attention.

Business commentators and many politicians have ignored the problems of working people by suggesting that since the unemployment rate remains lower than in the previous two recessions, the recent economic downturn has had only limited effects. Once we scratch the surface, however, we see that for many this downturn has been very painful. Over the last twenty years, it has become more difficult for unemployed workers to collect unemployment insurance, food stamps, welfare, or other government supports. As a result, the pain has been worsened by these government cutbacks that have left many without a safety net. There are signs of slowing wage growth, which indicate that the slack labor market is taking its toll even on those who are still employed. Cutbacks in the states in government services due to fiscal difficulties may only exacerbate the harshness of the current labor market downturn for millions of American families.

For women, this downturn meant more job losses than during the early 1990s. The sectors of the economy that generally help pull us out of a recession—services and retail trade—did not provide job growth this time around. For minority workers, the gains of the Clinton era may prove to be fragile as unemployment has shot up and employment rates have fallen. Most importantly, the rise in unemployment rates may not yet be over; economic growth in the second half of 2002 was much slower than expected and consumer confidence continues to erode. And even if unemployment begins to decline, there is no evidence of a commitment to accelerate economic growth in order to return to the low unemployment rates experienced at the peak of the Clinton-era economic boom.

The Economic Boom: What It Meant for Working Families

The late 1990s were a time of strong economic growth, and not just for those at dot-coms or with stock portfolios. The average worker saw wages rise by nearly 10 percent between 1995 and 2000, and, unlike in the economic expansion of the 1980s, low-wage workers—those with earnings in the bottom 40 percent of all wage earners and most likely to have less education—saw significant and sustained wage gains over this time period. While the average inflation-adjusted wage rate for all nonsupervisory workers rose by 7.3 percent, it rose by 9.8 percent for retail workers and, more generally, by more than 10.0 percent for both male and female workers in the lowest-paid decile of all workers.

The good economic years did not last long enough, however, to overcome the fall in wages since the late 1970s for those workers at the bottom. In 2001, wages for men and women at the tenth percentile of workers remained 2.6 and 2.2 percent below their 1979 levels, after adjusting for inflation. Further, not all jobs benefited from the boom: the real wages of manufacturing workers increased by only 3.8 percent between 1995 and 2000.

Strong wage gains followed from the tight labor market during the late 1990s. Official unemployment fell to 3.9 percent twice during 2000 and averaged 4.0 percent for the year. Critically, unemployment stayed low longer—without signs of inflation—than economists generally had thought possible. As with wage gains, low unemployment was shared across demographics groups: three times during 2000 (March, April, and September), the unemployment rate for African-Americans fell to 7.3 percent, the lowest since the Bureau of Labor Statistics (BLS) began tabulating unemployment separately by race in 1972. Indeed, from 1972 through 1997, African-American unemployment had never fallen below 10 percent. Hispanic unemployment also fell to a historic low of 5.7 percent in 2000.[1]

Along with low unemployment, the proportion of Americans employed grew to historic highs. Women and especially workers of color gained the most, although they started at a lower employment level than did white workers. Between 1992 and 2000, the employment rate for African-American and Hispanic women increased by 9.0 and 6.6 percentage points, respectively, while it increased by only 2.7 percentage points for white women. Single mothers in particular saw their employment rates rise dramatically: between 1996 and 2000, the employment rate of African-American and Hispanic single mothers increased by 12.5 and 16.1 percentage points, respectively, whereas it increased by only 5.7 percentage points for white single mothers (Levitan and Gluck 2002). Low unemployment, however, did not mean that every American had a job or that the racial disparity in access to jobs had been eradicated. While at historically low levels, the 2000 African-American unemployment rate (7.6 percent annually) remained more than double that of whites (3.5 percent annually).

The sustained racial difference in unemployment rates actually underestimates the employment difficulties that African-American men continued to face during the economic boom. Whereas 88.2 percent of white men and 89.8 percent of Hispanic men aged twenty to sixty-four were in the labor force (with a job or looking for work), for comparably aged African-American men, labor force participation was only 79.8 percent. As a result, though unemployment rates were at record low levels, the employment rate of African-American men in the second quarter of 2000 was no higher than it had been at the peak of the previous expansion a decade earlier. Relatively low labor force participation rates for African-American men—even during the peak of the economic boom—reflects a lack of jobs available for African-American men: it has been estimated that lack of jobs accounts for probably one-half of the racial labor force gap (Juhn 2000). If this estimate is correct, the official unemployment rate in 2000 missed more than half a million African-American men.[2]

The late 1990s was also a period of significant policy experimentation. In 1996, President Clinton signed the Personal Responsibility and Work Opportunity Reconciliation Act, commonly known as "welfare reform." Because of tight labor markets, 60 to 75 percent of women who left welfare—welfare leavers—worked at some point. Pay, however, was not enough to support a family: most welfare leavers found jobs paying $6 to $8 per hour (Loprest 2001). If they worked full-time, full-year at a $6 per hour job, their annual income would equal $12,480. Together with the earned income tax credit (EITC) and other transfer programs, many of these families would have just enough income to escape "official" poverty.[3] Unfortunately, as Boushey et al. (2001) document, the government estimate of the income sufficient for a family to escape poverty—$16,640 for a family of three—is woefully inadequate. Detailed budget studies for communities across the United States find that it takes between $21,989 (in rural Hattiesburg, Mississippi) and $48,606 (in high-priced Nassau and Suffolk counties, New York) to afford the basic necessities (including food, housing, health insurance, child care, transportation, and taxes). Thus, even with high employment levels and strong wage growth, most welfare leavers came nowhere near income levels necessary for them to avoid hardships like going without meals, having their utilities cut off, or facing housing evictions.

It is also important to bear in mind that higher employment rates can pose real dilemmas for families, especially those with young children. During the late 1990s, due in part to welfare reform, single mothers began to work more than married mothers. Between 1996 and 2000, the employment rate of married mothers remained constant at 68.3 percent of the working age population whereas for single mothers it rose from 65.9 to 75.5 percent. The contrast is even more striking when looking only at mothers with children under age six: the employment rate of those who were married fell from 61.0 to 59.9 percent while the employment rate of those who were unmarried rose from 55.2 to 69.1 percent.

Welfare reform compelled single mothers to find full-time jobs while families with young children and two parents were able to use some of the earnings gains from the Clinton-era expansion to reduce the wife's work effort. While some states did provide decent day care for low-income parents and those recently off welfare, too many single mothers had to accept unreliable and low quality sites for their young children. Further, government subsidies have been paltry at best: in 1999, only 12 percent of eligible families received assistance through the Child Care and Development Fund (Layzer and Collins 2001; U.S. Department of Human Services 1999).

The Recession: Nothing to Fall Back On

The business press generally acts as though the recession of the early twenty-first century was relatively shallow and is now over. However, as of fall 2003, unemployment has not begun to decline and remains at its high of 6.0 percent. Further, in some ways, this recession was deeper than that of the early 1990s. Most importantly, the proportion of Americans with a job—the employment rate—fell more during the recent downturn than the previous one. Workers in sectors hit hardest by the attacks on the World Trade Center and the Pentagon of September 11, 2001, such as transportation, retail sales, and services generally, have lost the most jobs. As a result, women have lost nearly as many jobs as have men, whereas usually in downturns, men see a much greater employment loss. Over the course of this downturn, however, minority youth have not seen their employment rates fall as much. This may indicate that the gains experienced by workers of color during the boom may not be entirely eroded by the downturn.

One indicator of the difficulties families are facing during this recent downturn is that growth in nominal wages has slowed, especially for workers at the bottom. For the one-year period ending the first quarter of 2001, among all nonsupervisory workers, wages grew at around 4.2 percent, but they grew by only 3.0 percent in the recent one-year period ending the first quarter of 2003. For retail workers, wage growth declined from 3.8 to 2.7 percent, while for manufacturing workers, it declined from 3.5 to 2.6 percent. In addition, wages of both female and male workers at the tenth percentile have fallen by half. Slower wage growth is likely to continue as long as unemployment remains high and economic growth remains weak.

Part of the reason that the commentators see this downturn as short and shallow is that they define a recession based on changes in national income and downplay labor market conditions. An alternative definition would be based on times when the unemployment rate is increasing. Using this alternative definition, the latest downturn began in the second half of 2000 even though total production, as measured by gross domestic product (GDP), did not begin to decline until the middle of 2001. When GDP began to grow in the first half of 2002, the business press declared the recession was over even though the unemployment rate continued to rise.

The downturn of the early 2000s has turned out to be the longest

Table 3.1

Underemployment (in thousands)

	2000 : I	2003 : I	Percent change
Civilian labor force	141,708	145,599	2.7
Unemployed	6,223	9,224	48.2
Underemployed:			
Marginally attached workers			
Discouraged	254	458	80.3
Other marginally attached	982	1,130	15.1
Involuntary part-time	3,426	4,993	45.7
Total underemployed	10,885	15,805	45.2

Source: U.S. Department of Labor, BLS. 2003. Current Population Survey. Washington, DC: Bureau of Labor Statistics (available at www.bls.gov/cps/home.htm).

period of sustained job losses since the Great Depression of the 1930s. During the previous downturn, which lasted two years, the unemployment rate of those twenty years and older grew by 2.1 percentage points, from 4.6 to 6.7 percent. During the recent downturn, measured through April 2003, the unemployment rate for the working-age population had grown by only 1.9 percentage points, from 3.3 to 5.2 percent.[4] Thus, the recent downturn had a smaller unemployment rate increase and the rate of unemployment remains substantially below the peak of the last downturn.

The somewhat smaller unemployment increase of the current downturn, however, obscures the true extent of joblessness. The unemployment rate calculated by the BLS excludes workers who are not fully employed or who would like to be employed but do not meet the government's job search requirement. A broader—but still incomplete—measure of "underemployment" is presented in Table 3.1. This alternative measure includes unemployed workers as well as (1) those working part-time but who want to work full-time ("involuntary" part-timers), (2) those who want to work but have been discouraged from searching by their lack of success ("discouraged" workers), and (3) others who are neither working nor seeking work at the moment but who indicate that they want and are available to work and have looked for a job in the last twelve months. Table 3.1 shows that during the latest downturn, the number of underemployed increased by about the same percentage as the number of officially unemployed. By the first quarter of 2003, the underemploy-

Table 3.2

Share of Unemployed Who Are Long-Term Unemployed (in percent)

	1990 : I	1992 : I	2000 : I	2003 : I
All	9.4	17.7	11.2	20.5
Men				
White	10.2	18.5	10.4	18.6
Black	14.4	21.8	19.5	28.5
Ratio	1.41	1.18	1.88	1.53
Women				
White	6.9	15.2	8.9	18.2
Black	8.8	16.1	13.3	25.0
Ratio	1.28	1.06	1.49	1.37

Source: U.S. Department of Labor, BLS. 2003. Current Population Survey. Washington, DC: Bureau of Labor Statistics, (available at www.bls.gov/cps/home.htm), Table A-35.

Note: Quarterly data computed from monthly data and not seasonally adjusted.

ment rate had increased by 3.1 percentage points to 10.7 percent of the labor force, affecting 15.8 million workers.

There have been other changes to the composition of the unemployed that indicate that this latest downturn is more severe than implied by the 6.0 percent unemployment rate. Table 3.2 measures the long-term unemployment rate: the share of those unemployed who are unemployed for more than six months. Note that at the peak of the most recent and past business cycle, the long-term unemployment rate of white men was virtually unchanged at 10.4 and 10.2 percent, respectively. By contrast, the long-term unemployment rate of black men rose from 14.4 to 19.5 percent, increasing the black-white ratio from 1.41 to 1.88. A similar pattern occurred among women, where the black-white ratio rose from 1.28 to 1.49. Thus, when measured peak-to-peak, there was a disproportionate growth of the long-term unemployment rate for black workers.

The long-term unemployment rate increases during economic downturns, more so for white workers during the recent economic downturn. Indeed, at the trough of the last downturn, the racial disparity was virtually eliminated. By contrast, at the present stage in the latest downturn, the share of long-term unemployed is higher than at any point in the last business cycle for both men and women, with more than one-quarter of unemployed African-American workers experiencing long-term unemployment. This data strongly suggests that for African-American workers, unemployment is a much more serious problem than in the previous downturn.

Table 3.3

Employment Rates for Workers Ages 20 to 64 (in percent)

	1990 : 1	1992 : 1	Percent change	2000 : 1	2003 : 1	Percent change
All	74.6	72.8	−1.9	76.8	74.3	−2.6
Men						
White	85.2	82.1	−3.1	85.2	81.9	−3.3
Black	73.3	69.0	−4.3	73.7	68.8	−4.9
Hispanic*	78.9	75.2	−3.7	85.8	82.4	−3.5
Women						
White	66.8	66.5	−0.2	70.8	69.4	−1.4
Black	62.9	59.9	−3.0	69.7	66.1	−3.6
Hispanic	52.2	50.0	−2.2	60.9	58.9	−2.1

* For Hispanics, 20 years and older.
Source: U.S. Department of Labor, BLS. 2003. *Current Population Survey.* Washington, DC: Bureau of Labor Statistics, (available at www.bls.gov/cps/home.htm), Table A-16.
Note: Data not seasonally adjusted.

The growth of long-term African-American unemployment should not be surprising. In the past, African-American workers would become discouraged and drop out of the labor force so that their long-term unemployment would not show up in official statistics.[5] Today, it is much less likely that they will drop out of the labor force when suffering long-term unemployment. With less labor market discrimination, they can be somewhat more optimistic; with less of a safety net available, they have little choice but to continue actively searching for a job.

There has also been a secular increase in the proportion of all women who are long-term unemployed. This is at least partially a result of women's increased attachment to the workforce: as women's income has become more important to families, when they lose a job, they have tended to stay in the labor force longer rather than dropping out.

The recent downturn also appears to be more severe when we examine changes in the employment rate—the proportion of people with a job—rather than the unemployment rate. As unemployment rises because people lose their jobs, the employment rate tends to fall. Whereas the employment rate for the working-age population fell by 1.9 percentage points over the 1990–1992 downturn, it has fallen by much more—2.6 percent points—during the latest downturn (Table 3.3).

For white men, the decline in employment rates during the recent downturn is essentially the same as during the previous downturn through the first quarter of 2003. By contrast, African-Americans and white women have seen their employment rates fall more during this last downturn than the previous downturn. For Hispanic workers, it appears that the latest downturn has been milder but this may be a result of changes in the weights used by the census to calculate Hispanic averages.

The composition of job losses during the recent downturn is partially a result of the terrorist attacks of September 11, which wreaked havoc on a few segments of the economy—air travel, hotels, and retail. Figure 3.1A shows how employment declined across industries pre– and post–September 2001. In the first eleven months of the downturn (October 2000 through September 2001), services continued to grow, adding 0.9 percent to payrolls, and transportation fell only slightly. However since September 2001, services have not grown at all, and transportation and wholesale and retail trade have experienced steeper employment declines.

For comparison purposes, Figure 3.1B breaks down the earlier downturn into the first eleven months and the remainder of the downturn. Unlike the second part of the 2000–2002 recession, during the second part of the earlier downturn, services grew by 2.8 percent and transportation and wholesale trade fell about the same as in the first eleven months. Retail trade actually grew in the latter part of the earlier downturn, as opposed to falling as it has in the latter part of the 2000–2002 downturn. It is likely that September 11 contributed to a deepening of the latest downturn in sectors that usually moderate employment difficulties.

Since many of the hardest hit sectors of the economy were those that disproportionately employ women, the effects of the events of September 11 on the labor market help to explain why African-American and white female employment declines in the recent downturn were larger than in previous downturns. In addition, the aftershocks of the terrorist attacks on the economy, in particular the effects on tourism and retail trade, altered the gender composition of employment declines as compared to previous recessions. During the early 1990s downturn, men experienced larger employment declines than did women. During the latest downturn, however, white women have begun to catch up with white men, while for African-American women this downturn caused a greater employment-rate decline than it did for African-American men.

Economic downturns are always harsh for young workers because

Figure 3.1A   Employment Change over 2000–2002 Recession, through July 2002 (in percent)

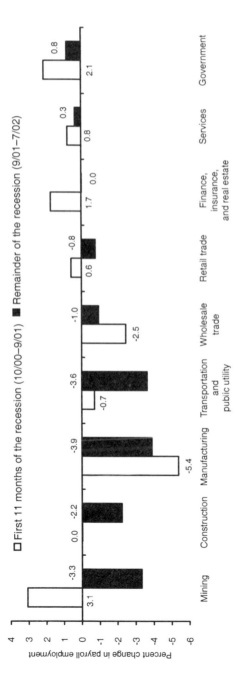

Source: Mishel, Bernstein, and Boushey (2002).

Figure 3.1B   **Employment Change over 1990–1992 Recession** (in percent)

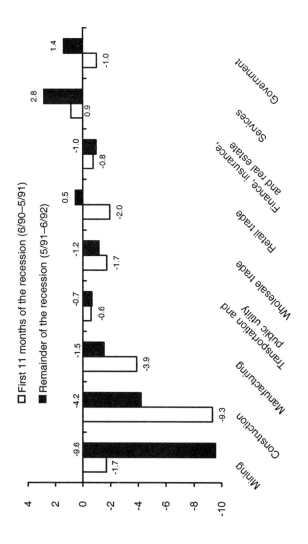

Source: Mishel, Bernstein, and Boushey (2003).

Table 3.4

Share of Out-of-School, High-School Graduates Working Full-Time
(in percent)

	1990 : I	1992 : I	Percent change	2000 : I	2003 : I	Percent change
All	76.3	70.0	−6.4	75.0	70.0	−5.0
No more than high school degree	73.2	66.0	−7.2	71.4	65.7	−5.8

Source: U.S. Department of Labor, BLS. 2003. *Current Population Survey*. Washington, DC: Bureau of Labor Statistics, (available at www.bls.gov/cps/home.htm), Table A-16.

employers can replace them with unemployed adults who are generally better trained and more reliable. This is even more the case for young workers with no more than a high school degree. As a result, the decline in full-time employment rates for out-of-school high-school graduates (Table 3.4) is more substantial than the employment rate declines experienced by the working-age population (Table 3.1). In addition, in both downturns there was a larger decline in the full-time employment rate among those with no more than a high school degree. However, this latest recession may not be as hard on youth workers as the one in the early 1990s. For the entire youth population, as well as for those with no more than a high school degree, the full-time employment rate has fallen slightly less during the recent downturn than it had in the previous downturn.

Table 3.5 indicates that the dramatic gains made during the Clinton expansion in the ability of young African-Americans to secure full-time employment have been sustained. The full-time employment rates of African-American men, African-American women, and African-Americans with no more than a high school degree have remained well above their levels of a decade earlier.

Policy Recommendations

The economic gains for those at the bottom of the labor market may be the most fragile. Typically in recession, unemployment rises more among less-paid workers and the proportional effect on earnings and family income is greater than it is for higher-paid workers (Mishel, Bernstein,

Table 3.5

Share of Out-of-School, 16-to-24-Year-Olds Working Full-Time
(in percent)

	1992 : I	2003 : I	Percent change
All	69.9	70.0	0.1
No more than high school			
White	68.7	68.0	−0.7
Black	51.5	54.2	2.7
Hispanic	68.1	71.9	3.8
Men			
White	73.3	74.5	1.2
Black	53.2	60.0	6.8
Hispanic	67.8	76.4	8.6
Women			
White	71.2	68.1	−3.1
Black	56.4	59.9	3.5
Hispanic	70.5	64.0	−6.4

Source: U.S. Department of Labor, BLS. 2003. *Current Population Survey.* Washington, DC: Bureau of Labor Statistics, (available at www.bls.gov/cps/home.htm), Table A-16.
Note: Data not seasonally adjusted.

and Boushey 2003). As we showed above, many workers had been struggling even during the boom. Job losses caused by the recession may require government to rethink recent policies that "get tough" on poor families and to evaluate how fiscal and monetary policy is affecting economic growth and changes in unemployment.

In order for the economy to pull itself out of this latest recession, economic growth must resume. However, it is not enough for growth to be positive; growth must be sufficient to absorb new labor market entrants and offset labor productivity increases. The labor force grows at about 1 percent per year and labor productivity currently is growing at about 2 percent annually. This implies that overall economic growth in the economy—growth in GDP—must be at least 3 percent annually for unemployment to fall. During the last two years, however, growth, while positive, has been insufficient to bring down unemployment. Thus, the economy has been experiencing a "jobless recovery" similar to what happened in the early 1990s, when unemployment continued to rise for eighteen months after the recession had been declared "officially" over.

But it is not enough for unemployment to fall just a little. In terms of policy, the first thing is to note that higher unemployment leads not only to job losses, but to wage stagnation. To return to the strong wage growth and high employment rates of the late 1990s, the unemployment rate must return to its previous lows of around 4.0 percent. For workers to benefit, the 1990s have shown that we need to see *sustained* low unemployment, lasting for a number of years. During the first three years of the Clinton-era expansion when unemployment hovered around 6 percent, there were few benefits for the most vulnerable workers.[6] It was only when the unemployment rate fell below 5 percent in 1997 that African-American men, welfare leavers, and those with less education gained higher wages and more secure employment. Thus, we should demand robust economic expansion rather than the slow recovery that the Federal Reserve favors.

This chapter has also pointed to additional problems specifically faced by the poorest Americans: inadequate incomes pose real risks for welfare leavers and their children. The 1996 welfare reform legislation implemented lifetime limits for welfare receipt that were arbitrarily set at five years. Some states have chosen to implement even shorter time limits. These limits are in effect regardless of the unemployment rate. Unfortunately, many welfare recipients use welfare as an unemployment insurance system: workers who earn little or who work part-time or intermittently are least likely to qualify for unemployment compensation and welfare may be their only option. At the most basic level, there should be a priority to improve access to safety net programs, including welfare and food stamps. Thus, we should demand that welfare lifetime limits be adjusted when the economy is weak so that these vulnerable families have access to needed benefits.

Critics of this approach claim that it is arbitrary to determine when the economy is too weak to expect welfare recipients to obtain paid employment. Is it when the unemployment rate is 5, 6, 7, or 8 percent? In addition, if months on welfare do not count toward lifetime limits, they fear it will send the wrong message and reverse the psychology that had allowed hundreds of thousands of recipients to gain stable employment during boom times.

Rather than picking one unemployment rate at which to stop the clock on lifetime limits, an alternative policy would be to develop a flexible relationship between lifetime limits and the state of the economy. Suppose that once the unemployment rate rises above 5 percent, each month on welfare would count a declining fraction of one month toward life-time limits. For example, the fraction could decline to one-half when the unemployment rate rises to 6 percent; that is, every month would count as only one-half a month toward lifetime limits. Then the fraction could decline more slowly to be one-quarter when the unemployment rate reaches 7 percent and to a minimum value of one-eighth at unemployment rates of 8 percent or higher.

This proposal does not eliminate discretionary judgments. Clearly the illustrative choices of starting to discount when the unemployment rate rises above 5 percent and having a minimum fraction of one-eighth reached at 8 percent are arbitrary. Legislation would have to establish when to start the discounting, the pace at which the fraction declines, and choice of the minimum fraction. These judgments are much more manageable, however, than any attempt to pick one unemployment threshold above which being on welfare would not count toward lifetime limits.

Another dilemma facing low-income families and welfare families is that during the boom years, many states increased funding for child care; and it was in the states that were the most generous that the benefits to welfare leavers were the most favorable. However, as the economy weakened, states began to cut back on these work supports (Neuberger 2002). These work supports, however, are often critical for mothers who are trying to balance work and family while holding down a low-wage job. As Levitan and Gluck (2002, 45) report:

> The supply of subsidized child care has not kept pace with the rise in single mother employment. The latest data show that only one in seven federally eligible children receives child care, and in New York City an estimated 100,000 eligible children under six years of age do not receive subsidies. Interviews conducted by Community Service Society in the South Bronx, indicate that three-quarters of respondents did not receive transitional child care benefits within the first year of leaving public assistance; consequentially 15 percent reported losing their newly found jobs and 49 percent jeopardized their employment. Increasing the Child Care and Development Fund is essential. Increasing flexibility in the TANF block grant would also improve childcare quality, choice and access.

Maintaining funding for work supports programs is critical, especially during the economic downturn. Without these services, families that have moved from welfare to work may not be able to maintain employment. Further, such funding would provide much-needed economic stimulus.

Finally, policies should be promoted to allow those welfare leavers who are sustaining full-time employment to distance themselves from poverty. Few readers of this volume need to be convinced that these welfare leavers would benefit from minimum wage and/or living wage legislation. Single heads of households will find out, however, that increases in their market earnings do not translate into significant increases in take-home pay. As earnings increase, the federal government will tax the additional income and reduce the EITC. For each additional $100 earned, the Internal Revenue Service will take back $31 to $15 in additional taxes and $16 in reduced credits. Families with two children lose $21 in credits for every $100 in additional income and many face the same $15 in additional taxes, so that for these families, $36 goes back to the federal government. Even after the sizable benefits to low-income families from the 2001 tax legislation is fully phased in, about one-fifth of all families with children and annual incomes below $40,000 will still face a combined rate of at least 26 percent.

When we add additional payroll and state taxes, and potential losses of food stamps, housing, and child care subsidies, government tax and transfer policies severely limit the ability of single heads of households to distance themselves from poverty thresholds. In Wisconsin, if a single mother with two children sees her annual wages increase from $15,000 to $20,000, her disposable income would only increase by $1,840—an implicit tax rate of 63.2 percent. As a result, policies to reduce the implicit tax rate faced by the working poor should be an important component of antipoverty proposals. One such policy is the simplified family credit promoted by the Economic Policy Institute (Cherry and Sawicky 2001).

Conclusion

Welfare proposals that increase the ability of single mothers to balance full-time work with family responsibilities are something that one would expect compassionate conservatives to embrace. Indeed, recognition of the difficulties inherent in balancing single parenthood with full-time employment has been the reason why work supports have had widespread support among even Republican governors. Similarly, the attempt to lower the implicit tax rate faced by the working poor should find favor with conservatives who rail against the disincentives of the allegedly high tax rates faced by the wealthy. However, as commentator

Arianna Huffington has made clear, George W. Bush abandoned his initial posture as a compassionate conservative long ago and instead has adopted a mean-spirited approach, exemplified by his attempt to lengthen the workfare requirement from thirty to forty hours per week and restrict still further the ability of those on welfare to substitute schooling for work requirements. Nor has he shown any inclination to focus on the working poor. Instead, he focused on the "pain" experienced by those whose stock portfolios have gone south, floating the idea of tax law changes that would allow them to deduct more of their losses from taxable income (Gale and Orszag 2002).

Our demand that federal legislation be enacted to stimulate a rapid expansion would have been a consensus approach of Democrats forty years ago. Given the success of the Keynesian-inspired Kennedy tax cut, there was widespread acceptance of the beneficial effects of deficit spending when the economy is weak. Indeed, even the patriarch of conservative economists, Milton Friedman, sarcastically commented, "We are all Keynesians now." Of course, starting with his 1968 American Economics Association presidential address, Friedman began the counterattack on Keynesianism. This counterattack grew in the 1970s, as younger economists—enamored of concepts of rational expectations and crowding out—were won to the anti-Keynesian side, and it became triumphant with the ascendancy of Robert Rubin in the Clinton administration. And now Krugman (2002) concretizes this rout: after indicating how weak the economy is, he explicitly rejects his long-held Keynesian view that "there is plenty of room for fiscal stimulus." Thus, one of the more depressing aspects of the current situation is: Where are the compassionate conservatives and where are the Keynesian Democrats?

The fall 2003 beginning of a robust expansion may lull George W. Bush into believing that he will not pay a political price for neglecting the domestic economy. This recent downturn did not appear to be deep, but for many who lost their jobs the current expansion brings little comfort. Even another year of continued robust economic growth is unlikely to lower the unemployment rate below 5 percent, still quite distant from the lower rates experienced during the last two years of the Clinton-era boom. As a result, many working people are unlikely to have their incomes return by the 2004 election to the levels they experienced before the downturn. Most telling, the Federal Reserve has indicated its desire to slow down the expansion because of inflation fears so that unemployment rates of 5.0 to 5.5 percent will again become the acceptable level.

Thus, Bush should consider carefully the damage done to working Americans and support growth policies that will carry the expansion still further if he hopes to gain their support.

Notes

1. For more evidence on the impact of the expansion on various labor groups, see Mishel, Bernstein, and Boushey (2003) and Cherry (2001).

2. The official unemployment rate includes only individuals in the noninstitutionalized population. There are 20 percent more women than men in the noninstitutionalized African-American population aged twenty to sixty-four years old, but only 1 percent more white women than white men. For the African-American gender ratio to equal the white ratio, there would have to be 1.75 million more African-American men in the noninstitutionalized populations. Where are these "missing" men? Largely in prisons, thanks to the "war against drugs." Since many of these incarcerated black men would be unemployed, there is another large group that is left out of the official unemployment statistics.

3. Levitan and Gluck (2002) found that among working single mothers from 1999 to 2001, 36.5 percent did not earn enough to escape poverty through their wages alone. Once government transfer payments were included, however, only 14.2 percent had incomes below the official poverty line.

4. Note that by excluding teenagers, unemployment rates for the working-age population are consistently lower than for the entire labor market.

5. This was especially the case for young African-Americans. For example, in 1982, during the most severe postwar downturn, only 8 percent of sixteen- to twenty-four-year-olds showed up as long-term unemployed. However, Freeman and Medoff (1982) used the same data to show that 21 percent of out-of-school black men ages twenty to twenty-four had no work experience in the previous year.

6. For example, the unemployment rate of African-American men fell between 1993 and 1996, but most of the decline reflected more African-American men dropping out of the labor force, so that their employment rate barely increased (Cherry 2000).

References

Boushey, Heather, Chaura Brocert, Bethney Gundersen, and Jared Bernstein. 2001. *Hardship in America: The Real Story of Working Families*. Washington, DC: Economic Policy Institute.

Cherry, Robert. 2000. "Impact of Tight Labor Markets on Black Employment." *Review of Black Political Economy* 27, no. 2: 27–41.

———. 2001. "African-Americans and the Social Benefits of Tight Labor Markets." *Working USA* 5, no. 2 (Fall): 106–18.

Cherry, Robert, and Max Sawicky. 2001. "And Now for Something Completely Different: Progressive Tax Cuts That Republicans Can Support." *Challenge* 44, no. 3 (May/June): 43–60.

Freeman, Richard, and James Medoff. 1982. "The Youth Labor Market Problem." In

The Youth Labor Market Problem, ed. Richard Freeman and David Wise, pp. 3–20. Chicago: University of Chicago Press.

Gale, William, and Peter Orszag. 2002. "A New Round of Tax Cuts?" Brookings Institution, working paper, 22 August.

Juhn, Chinhui. 2000. "Black-White Employment Differential in a Tight Labor Market." In *Prosperity for All? The Economic Boom and African-Americans*, ed. Robert Cherry and William Rodgers, pp. 88–109. New York: Russell Sage.

Krugman, Paul. 2002. "Minding the Gap." *New York Times*, 16 August, A 17.

Layzer, Jean I., and Ann Collins. 2001. "Access to Child Care for Low-Income Working Families Report." Washington, DC: U.S. Department of Health and Human Services.

Levitan, Mark, and Robin Gluck. 2002. *Mothers' Work: Single Mothers' Employment, Earnings, and Poverty in the Age of Welfare Reform*. New York: Community Service Society of New York.

Loprest, Pamela. 2001. *How Are Families That Left Welfare Doing? A Comparison of Early and Recent Welfare Leavers*. Research Report B-36. Washington, DC: Urban Institute.

Mishel, Lawrence, Jared Bernstein, and Heather Boushey. 2003. *The State of Working America 2002–2003*. Ithaca, NY: Cornell University Press.

Neuberger, ZoN. 2002. *States Are Already Cutting Child Care and TANF-Funded Programs*. Washington, DC: Center on Budget and Policy Priorities.

U.S. Department of Human Services. 1999. *National Study of Child Care for Low-Income Families*. Washington, DC: U.S. Department of Human Services.

II

Workers and Workforce Issues

4

A Report from the Front Lines of Welfare Reform

Fran Bernstein and Cecilia Perry

Much has been written about the impact welfare reform has had on aid recipients. Far less has been published concerning welfare reform's profound implications for the tens of thousands of front-line workers who administer the Temporary Assistance for Needy Families (TANF) and related programs.[1] Many of these welfare workers have made the difficult transition from solely determining eligibility for cash assistance to being multitasked TANF caseworkers. The American Federation of State, County and Municipal Employees (AFSCME) represents a significant segment of these human services workers. This chapter documents the new workplace challenges they face.

AFDC to TANF: A New World for Caseworkers

Aid to Families with Dependent Children (AFDC) was an entitlement program that paid monthly cash benefits to all financially eligible families. Under AFDC, eligibility workers reviewed income documentation, determined a family's eligibility, and issued benefit checks. Work-related requirements for AFDC were much more flexible than under TANF, with most recipients engaged in education, training, and job search (Bloom 1997). Moreover, eligibility workers were not expected to move clients out of AFDC within a certain period of time because it was not a time-limited program; families could receive cash assistance as long as they remained financially eligible.

TANF abolished the entitlement to cash assistance and with it the federal-state match that financed welfare payments and services. States now receive fixed federal block grant funding that does not change according to the number of eligible families. Further, TANF requires states to have a certain percentage of adult recipients participating in prescriptive, "countable" work activities for a fixed number of hours per week. States must terminate federal financial assistance to families within a lifetime limit of five years.

Caseload Declines

One of the hallmarks of welfare reform has been the dramatic decline in TANF caseloads since the mid-1990s. Between August 1996 and June 2000, TANF caseloads declined by 53 percent nationwide (U.S. Department of Health and Human Services 2002). (While researchers continue to debate what percentage of caseload decline was due to the strong economy rather than welfare reform policies, it is indisputable that the 10 percent employment growth in the late 1990s contributed substantially to the decline in caseloads.) During the recent recession, the national caseload fell 3 percent from March 2001 to December 2002, but more states reported caseload increases than decreases (Center on Law and Social Policy 2003).

TANF caseload decline has not necessarily translated into fewer cases for human services workers, however. Leaving TANF is not synonymous with escaping poverty. Poor families, whether receiving TANF assistance or not, often continue to qualify for food stamps and Medicaid. And, even as some former TANF recipients have entered low-wage employment, their wages are often so low that many continue to qualify for subsidized child care, child nutrition programs, transportation assistance, and other government supports.

Workload Increases

In the TANF era, the amount of work required for each case has much greater significance for understanding TANF caseworkers' jobs than a simple tally of cases per caseworker. Almost without exception, AFSCME-member caseworkers report that their workloads have increased dramatically since the advent of welfare reform. While caseworkers are still expected to determine eligibility, they also conduct extensive client interviews, develop individualized employment plans, identify barriers to employment, track clients' progress, refer clients to myriad support services and employment-related programs, and ensure that clients are complying with federal, state, and in some cases county rules concerning work requirements and time limits.

AFSCME's Council 31, which represents thousands of TANF caseworkers throughout the state of Illinois, has documented this trend. In a 1998 survey of its TANF caseworker members, Council 31 found that job duties increased significantly for almost all employees after welfare reform. Some 90 percent of front-line workers saw their workloads increase, with 53 percent reporting that their workloads grew by over 40 percent. More than 73 percent of caseworkers reported they had at least four new duties added to their jobs since the advent of welfare reform; 30 percent had more than eight new duties added (AFSCME Council 31 1999).

This increased workload phenomenon is not unique to Illinois. In Indiana, AFSCME's Council 62, in a joint project with the Indiana Administration of Public Assistance Programs, Division of Family and Children, established a TANF workload weighting system. Each job duty is assigned a numerical weight established in points, and each TANF caseworker (called family case coordinator) is expected to have a workload in the range of 60 to 80 points. Council 62 staff recently reported that family case coordinators in Indiana have workloads averaging 175 points, and in Marion County—where Indianapolis is located —family case coordinators average 220 points.

In focus groups held in Baltimore in 2001, AFSCME-represented TANF caseworkers spoke about feeling overwhelmed by greatly increased, and more complex, workloads. One Baltimore caseworker explained, "We're trying to do two jobs at once. We're trying to provide cash assistance and we're trying to provide job assistance." In fact, the focus group participants were hard-pressed to name any improvements in their own jobs since welfare reform (Kiley and Company 2001).

AFSCME is not the only organization that has documented the TANF workload explosion. The Texas-based Center for Public Policy Priorities found that the average time for an eligibility interview increased from 50 to 90 minutes, while staffing declined by at least 12 percent (Center for Public Policy Priorities 2001). And the Rand Corporation found that the workload for CalWORKs (California's welfare reform program) eligibility workers increased for four reasons: (1) working recipients require about twice as much effort as nonworking recipients; (2) CalWORKs imposed several new eligibility requirements, all of which caseworkers must verify; (3) noncompliant cases have expanded as more requirements have been imposed; and (4) work requirements were imposed for a higher percentage of the caseload (Rand Corporation 2000).

Demands on caseworkers have become heavier recently because families remaining on the TANF caseload tend to have significant and often multiple barriers to employment. These include low educational attainment, an ill or disabled family member, domestic violence in the home, substance or alcohol abuse problems, and/or mental health issues. A Baltimore focus group participant noted that the "hard core" keep on coming because they are not able to work (Kiley and Company 2001).

Indeed, increased workloads have become a central issue in collective bargaining agreements negotiated by AFSCME. In addition to Council 62's workload weighting system in Indiana, Council 31 in Illinois holds monthly labor-management meetings on caseloads, with additional staff brought in when needed, and AFSCME Local 61's contract with the state of Nebraska restricts mandatory imposition of additional open cases on staff and authorizes the use of overtime to handle added cases.

Increased Paperwork Burden

TANF caseworkers not only have to perform a large and broad array of new tasks, they must document them. An AFSCME member who is a supervisor in an upstate New York TANF office with thirty-one years' seniority laments the one to two hours per day he and the caseworkers he supervises now spend on paperwork. This includes new coding requirements that he believes have become more important than helping people. Now that several New York State departments are involved in welfare reform, supervisors and caseworkers have to fulfill the disparate requirements of each and fill out different forms for each.

Similarly, a caseworker in rural Pope County, Illinois, reports that the increased emphasis on paperwork makes it impossible for her colleagues and her to retain the "personal touch" that has worked so well in her community. Caseworkers in Marion County, Indiana, no longer have time to really work with families because of the mounting paperwork.

Insufficient Training

Further exacerbating the difficulties TANF caseworkers face, state and county administrators have generally failed to provide the training case-

workers need to maximize their effectiveness. While veteran caseworkers acknowledge that inadequate training was a problem in the old AFDC
program, it has grown in significance with the advent of new and changing rules and policies under welfare reform.

Caseworkers reported in the Council 31 survey that new employees
often receive little more than on-the-job training, which explains in part
why the Illinois Department of Human Services has a 30 percent turnover rate among first-year employees (AFSCME Council 31 1999).

Even veteran caseworkers express the need for more and better training, given all the new expectations placed upon them. One focus group
participant in Chicago derided "downtown training," saying, "That's a
joke. That's a waste. They teach you policy, but when you get to your
office, it's apples and oranges. They tell you what to do in theory. It's
got nothing to do with what you do when a real client comes in." A focus
group member in Baltimore noted, "With new policies and procedures,
we don't get the training until six months after it's needed." One result is
that caseworkers often are not familiar with the full scope of clients'
rights and benefits.

In short, new and better training programs must be developed. Efforts
are being undertaken at the federal level to address the dearth of staff
training and career development for TANF caseworkers. AFSCME, the
National Association of Social Workers, the Children's Defense Fund,
and other organizations are supporting new TANF requirements for ensuring a qualified and stable workforce. Among those recommendations
is the creation of a new grant program to help states provide comprehensive staff training and lower workloads.

Escalating Tension and Job Stress

TANF requirements, insufficient training, and overwhelming workloads
often combine to produce a volatile situation in TANF offices. Some
caseworkers have been pressured to enforce harsh rules for work participation and time limits. AFSCME employees in Illinois reported in a
2001 survey that they were directed by their supervisors to take adverse
actions contrary to agency policy. These members reported that their
supervisors appeared to feel under pressure to reduce caseloads, even if
that meant discouraging clients from accessing benefits or services. In
fact, 44 percent of the survey respondents reported that they had been
directed to take inappropriate actions in violation of agency policy in

handling a case. Moreover, 23 percent reported being pressured to meet a caseload quota (AFSCME Council 31 2001).

Not surprisingly, morale has been affected in TANF offices. Focus group members in Baltimore and Chicago described their managers and supervisors fostering an atmosphere of "near panic." They also referred to pressure to "meet the numbers" required for work participation and caseload reductions. The above-mentioned supervisor in upstate New York attributed his staff's occasional lack of sensitivity to "battle fatigue." Caseworkers in Indiana report that they have insufficient time to develop jobs for their clients and that they sometimes feel like "cattle herders."

Anxious clients who have trouble contacting their overworked caseworkers often perceive them as mean-spirited and uncaring. Not surprisingly, this dynamic has sometimes resulted in verbal abuse and violence in TANF offices. TANF caseworkers in New York City reported at least 150 violent incidents in welfare offices between mid-1998 and mid-2002 (Roberts 2002).

Changes in Welfare Delivery Systems Challenge Clients and Workers

In addition to high caseloads and workloads, TANF caseworkers and clients must adjust to constantly changing technologies and service delivery systems. For example, in many states TANF is now coordinated with workforce development agencies established under the Workforce Investment Act (WIA). Obviously, the goal is facilitating employment potential for clients. In some WIA One-Stop centers offering job placement assistance and employment and training-related services, TANF workers are co-located with other WIA caseworkers, integrating service delivery and facilitating clients' applications for many different services with a trip to one office.

On the other hand, extensive privatization in some One-Stops has weakened job placement and other services. Few public welfare agencies significantly expanded their in-house capacity to implement TANF work requirements. Instead, many welfare agencies have contracted with nonprofits and for-profit companies located off-site.

Call Centers

Cost-saving measures can take a toll on caseworkers' personal interactions with clients. Some states now operate call centers where caseworkers give information on case status or, in the case of unemployment compensation, take applications over the telephone, effectively blunting the personal interaction between clients and their caseworkers. Florida plans to use call centers for Medicaid eligibility determination, with the expectation of extending them to all social services.

The interaction between clients and caseworkers becomes more complicated when the call center is located in another country. Some states have contracted out their call center functions to eFunds, an Arizona-based company that subcontracts with companies based in India. When a state legislator in New Jersey discovered that workers in India were answering calls from welfare recipients, she proposed a bill to prohibit such contracts. New Jersey officials finally reached an agreement with eFunds to move the work back to New Jersey, but had to pay an additional $1.2 million for the contract change. The eFunds Bombay operation provides telephone assistance to welfare and food stamp recipients in 19 states (Waldman 2003).

Privatization Is a Constant Threat to TANF Workers

Proponents of privatization argue that it does everything but cure the common cold. The record of privatization is another matter. The 1996 welfare law permitted states to contract out to private companies eligibility determination for TANF cash assistance, a major change from AFDC, which required public employees to determine eligibility for cash benefits. Most states have maintained public administration for benefits but have contracted out many TANF-funded services (GAO 2002).

The most demoralizing threat to publicly employed TANF caseworkers comes from privatization. Dedicated caseworkers who have spent years in the public system assisting low-income families can be summarily laid off when services are contracted out. Some may be close to retirement and have difficulty replacing their salaries, health insurance coverage, and other benefits.

States facing fiscal crises often promote privatization as a solution. Under the guise of saving money, states contract out public services to private companies, but the savings, if any, often come from reductions in workers' wages and benefits. Employees who lose their jobs to privatization are often worse off if they accept a job with the contractor. Additionally, it is questionable that privatization does save money. After low-balling initial bids, contractors often increase contract costs in subsequent years (AFSCME 2002).

Wisconsin Contractors Increase Profits at Clients' Expense

Wisconsin was the first state to experiment with privatization of eligibility determination for cash assistance and the results have been controversial. Wisconsin Works, known as W-2, requires almost all adult welfare recipients to work. Milwaukee County, with 85 percent of the state's welfare population, awarded contracts to five private agencies to administer W-2. The private agencies reaped more than $25.2 million in profits between 1997 and 1999 (AFSCME Legislative Council 2000).

In the first round of contracts, the W-2 private agencies received fiscal incentives to reduce caseloads or services to clients because profits were directly related to the surplus the agency generated. The contracts lacked oversight and contained weak performance measures and accountability standards (AFSCME Legislative Council 1998).

W-2's structure actually encourages contractors to deny services or provide reduced services. Applicants who are not "job ready" receive W-2 services including community service assignments, transportation, and child care assistance. Contractors save money by reducing the type and number of services. For example, workers can assign applicants to community service rather than provide educational or training opportunities. When contractors reduce or deny services, they cut contract expenses and can claim some of this surplus as profits. In contrast, when a public agency reduces services, the "profit" remains in the public domain (AFSCME Legislative Council 1998).

W-2 privatization played a major role in reducing the food stamp and Medicaid rolls in Milwaukee. In theory, applicants denied W-2 services were referred to county workers for eligibility determination for food stamps and Medicaid. County workers were located with the private contractors for this purpose, but the private contractors did not consistently refer people to the county workers. Exacerbating this problem was the state's "light touch" policy that discouraged caseworkers from informing clients about other benefits they might have been eligible for, including food stamps and Medicaid (Wisconsin Department of Workforce Development n.d.).

In May 2003, approximately 140 Milwaukee County food stamp workers were moved out of the regional, private W-2 offices into a central office because the county budget is insufficient to pay for rent, computers, furniture, and security ("W-2 Workers Handling Food Stamps Will Move to One Office" 2003). This change will make it more difficult for W-2 applicants to apply for Medicaid and food stamps.

W-2 contractor abuses have been well documented. The Wisconsin Legislative Audit Bureau uncovered financial misdeeds, including using TANF funds for staff parties, Hollywood entertainers, expensive lunches for executives, and first-class air travel while these contractors were imposing harsh sanctions on welfare families for noncompliance with minor program rules. One contractor, Maximus, used W-2 TANF funds to market its services and generate business in New York, California, and Arizona (Wisconsin Legislative Audit Bureau 2001).

More recently, a nonprofit agency was fined $168,500 for improperly assigning W-2 status, delaying benefits, and improperly reducing benefits (Shultze 2003). The Milwaukee County W-2 Monitoring Task Force found that sixty-three cents of every dollar spent on W-2 paid for administrative expenses, and the task force criticized W-2 executives' annual salaries of $146,000 to $180,000 in 2000 (Shultze 2002).

Florida Proposes Contractors Provide All Government-Funded Services

In his January 2003 State of the State speech, given on the steps of the Florida Capitol, surrounded on all sides by state buildings with thousands of employees, Florida governor Jeb Bush declared, "There would be no greater tribute to our maturity as a society than if we can make these buildings around us empty of workers; silent monuments to the time when government played a larger role than it deserved or could adequately fill" (Wallsten 2003).

Bolstering Governor Bush's vision of disappearing government, the U.S. Department of Agriculture approved a Florida waiver to privatize food stamps eligibility in pilot programs operating in six counties (O'Neil 2002). This is the first time in the history of federal entitlement programs that for-profit corporations will determine eligibility for benefits. Florida expects to include eligibility for TANF and Medicaid in the same program, which requires a Medicaid waiver, with the goal of eventually expanding the pilots statewide in five years (Florida Agency for Health Care Administration 2003).

On a parallel track, Florida is experimenting with privatization of

Medicaid eligibility in its "2–1–1" system. The Federal Communications Commission designated the telephone number 2–1–1 as a national community information and referral service for health care, human services, economic assistance, crisis intervention, transportation, domestic violence, disability, mental health, substance abuse, and child welfare services. The United Way has established 2–1–1 systems in various parts of the country, including Florida.

Florida plans to expand its 2–1–1 information and referral system to include determination of eligibility for Medicaid and other social services. Florida submitted an application in April 2003 to the U.S. Department of Health and Human Services (HHS) for a Medicaid waiver to operate a 2–1–1 privatized pilot in ten counties before expanding statewide (Florida Agency for Health Care Administration 2003). HHS is expected to grant Florida's waiver request.

Not surprisingly, government workers in Florida feel under siege. Their unions continue to oppose privatization and most state workers have kept their jobs by filling vacancies in other departments. However, Florida's rapidly shrinking state government will limit transfer opportunities.

Not all TANF caseworkers view privatization as an imminent threat. In the Chicago focus group, AFSCME caseworkers viewed privatization as a long-term rather than an immediate threat (probably because of strong union protections) but were very critical of the vendors' performance in providing job training and job-placement services. Caseworkers questioned the basic qualifications of the private contractors, characterized them as "do-little or do-nothing companies," and reported having been pressured to refer clients to specific vendors (Kiley and Company 2001).

Enforcing Clients Rights Under a Privatized System

In Wisconsin, we observed that privatization can and does lead to wrongful limitations on clients' access to welfare benefits. These limitations involve clients' constitutional due process rights under well-established law. Unfortunately, privatization can also lead to wrongful denial of this same constitutional right. Lawyers in Florida representing welfare clients are concerned about application of constitutional due process rights when services are contracted out. Workforce Florida, the entity operating the Florida welfare program, is a private, nonprofit corporation. Due process requires welfare agencies to give welfare recipients notice of action taken pertaining to their benefits and the opportunity for a fair hearing. However, Workforce Florida does not require regional workforce boards to give clients notice or a fair hearing to contest decisions (Huddleston and Greenfield 2002).

Privately administered welfare program staff often are not familiar with the concept of due process, in contrast to workers in public agencies who are acutely aware of the importance and legal implications of denial of due process rights. Public agencies have procedures to enforce these rights, in contrast to private for-profit agencies unfamiliar with the procedural protections and whose decisions can be influenced by their desire to maximize profits.

Impact of States' Fiscal Crises

Almost uniformly, states are struggling with their worst fiscal crises since World War II. To balance their budgets, many states have reduced spending for social services programs, including TANF. At an AFSCME national conference in March 2003, members reported staff reductions, layoffs, unfilled vacancies, speed-up, forced overtime, increased outsourcing of their work, and workers replaced by clients participating in workfare programs (welfare recipients working in exchange for their welfare checks). Ironically, in New York City's attempt to balance its budget in spring 2003, several hundred of the municipal workers laid off had previously been on public assistance (as estimated by the president of AFSCME's clerical workers' local) (Greenhouse 2003).

The weak economy and the relatively high unemployment rate have exacerbated TANF workplace problems. Once upon a time, government strengthened its economic safety net when job losses led to more reliance on public assistance. Today, some governors are actually reducing their budgets for public assistance, fraying the safety net just when it is needed most.

In Denver, for example, Medicaid and food stamp caseloads increased to nearly 1,000 per caseworker in April 2003 (Schoettler 2003). Early in 2003, Connecticut's Governor John Rowland closed six social service offices to reduce the state budget deficit. A federal judge declined to block the closings, even though both staff and clients argued that larger caseloads would result in less attention for clients and that the closings would cause particular hardships for physically or mentally disabled clients who face challenges in traveling to distant offices (Fillo 2003).

AFSCME Council 31 in Illinois documented in 2002 how office clos-ings, employee layoffs, and early retirements are devastating staffing in TANF and related human services programs and leaving the remaining employees with even more crushing workloads (AFSCME Council 31 2002). And in California, which faces the most devastating state budget crisis, the state's chapter of the National Association of Social Workers reported, "Social Services and Public Welfare Services took the biggest hit in the form of reduced funding for the provision of services" (Peleg 2003).

TANF Program Policies

To some degree, TANF caseworkers share the general public's mixed views on the policies embodied in welfare reform itself. In the AFSCME focus groups in Baltimore and Chicago, most participants supported the general concept of time limits but believed that more exceptions should be allowed, especially for completing educational programs and drug treatment.

Caseworkers are committed to helping their clients escape poverty. How-ever, rigid numerical quotas for meeting federally imposed work require-ments often frustrate TANF workers when they cannot offer their clients options, especially education and training, that they believe are needed for families to succeed in the long run. Services to address serious barriers to employment, including drug and alcohol treatment and mental health services, often are not available when they are needed. And, increasingly, caseworkers say that the jobs to place clients in are just not there.

Ironically, some welfare policies directly threaten caseworkers' jobs. The largest threat is outsourcing TANF eligibility determinations, case-work, and services. Increased and overly prescriptive work requirements have also adversely affected some TANF caseworkers. For example, in some TANF programs, clients have been placed into workfare slots in TANF offices themselves, replacing vacant, full-time unionized posi-tions. We even know of occasions where laid-off public sector workers who went on welfare were placed in workfare slots doing the same jobs they had performed as public employees.

Conclusion

TANF caseworkers are in many ways the shock troops of welfare re-form. They do their best to implement laws, regulations, and policies that they had no real hand in developing and with which they may disagree. If caseworkers are to have a chance in helping their clients achieve their goal of a better and more economically secure life, the problems we have identified must be addressed. Caseworkers desperately need relief through realistic workloads, upgraded technology, reduced paperwork, more and better training, agency support, effective labor/management committees, and job security.

Note

1. There are approximately 100,000 front-line TANF workers and employment and training specialists in the United States (Annie E. Casey Foundation 2003, 44).

References

American Federation of State, County and Municipal Employees. 2002. *Safety Net for Sale.* Washington, DC.
American Federation of State, County and Municipal Employees Council 31. 1999. *Overworked and Underserved: A Report on the Status of the Illinois TANF Program for Caseworkers and Clients.* Executive Summary, January.
———. 2001. "Council 31 Community Operations Survey." August 8.
———. 2002. "A Disaster in the Making: How DHS Budget Cuts Are Placing Illinois Families in Jeopardy." October.
American Federation of State, County and Municipal Employees Legislative Council. 1998. *Private Profits, Public Needs: The Administration of W-2 in Milwaukee.* Madison, Wisconsin.
———. 2000. *Private Profits, Public Needs: The Administration of W-2 in Milwaukee.* Madison, Wisconsin.
Annie E. Casey Foundation. 2003. *The Unsolved Challenge of System Reform: The Condition of the Frontline Human Services Workforce.* Baltimore: Annie E. Casey Foundation.
Bloom, Dan. 1997. *After AFDC: Welfare-to-Work Choices and Challenges for States.* New York: Manpower Demonstration Research Corporation.
Center on Law and Social Policy. 2003. "Welfare Caseloads Increase in Most States in Fourth Quarter." *CLASP Update* 16, no. 5, May.
Center for Public Policy Priorities. 2001. "Further Cuts to DHS Staff Unjustifiable." *The Policy Page,* no. 114 (9 February).
Fillo, Maryellen. 2003. "Judge Declines to Block Closings." *Hartford Courant*, 22 January, B7.
Florida Agency for Health Care Administration. 2003. "2–1–1 HHS Eligibility Determination Project: An 1115 Waiver Research and Demonstration Proposal." April.
GAO. 2002. *Federal Oversight of State and Local Contracting Can Be Strengthened.* GAO 02–661. Washington, DC: Government Accounting Office.
Greenhouse, Steven. 2003. "From Work to Welfare? Reversal Feared in City Layoffs." *New York Times*, 21 May, B1.

Huddleston, Cindy, and Valory Greenfield. 2002. "Privatization of TANF in Florida: A Cautionary Tale." National Center on Poverty Law *Clearinghouse Review* 35, no. 9/10 (January/February): 540–45.

Kiley and Company. 2001. *TANF Focus Group Findings.* 6 June.

O'Neil, Bonnie. Acting Deputy Administrator, Food Stamp Program. 2002. Letter to Judge Kathleen A. Kearney, 7 July.

Peleg, Dori. 2003. "Some Way, Some How." *Dollars & Sense*, no. 247 (May/June): 24–26.

Rand Corporation. 2000. *Implementing CalWORKs: The Need for Added Capacity.* Rand Statewide CalWORKs Evaluation Research Brief RB-5040.

Roberts, Lillian. 2002. Executive Director, AFSCME District Council 37, June.

Schoettler, Gail. 2003. "First Victims of Economic Downturn." *Denver Post*, 6 April, E5.

Shultze, Steve. 2002. "Study Questions Cost Effectiveness of W-2." *Milwaukee Journal Sentinel*, 21 December, B3.

———. 2003. "Agency Fined $168,500 for Cutting W-2 Clients Short: State Audit Finds Mishandling of Cases in Northwest Milwaukee." *Milwaukee Journal Sentinel*, 24 March, B7.

U.S. Department of Health and Human Services, Administration for Children and Families. 2002. "Change in TANF Caseloads Since Enactment of New Welfare Law." 6 June. Available at www.acf.dhhs.gov/news/stats/aug-dec.htm.

Waldman, Amy. 2003. "More 'Can I Help You?' Jobs Migrate from U.S. to India." *New York Times*, 11 May, Section 1, 4.

Wallsten, Peter. 2003. "Bush Envisions Small Role for Government in Future." *Miami Herald*, 8 January, A1.

Wisconsin Department of Workforce Development. n.d. *Wisconsin Works Manual.*

Wisconsin Legislative Audit Bureau. 2001. *An Evaluation: Wisconsin Works W-2 Program: Department of Workforce Development.* Rep. 01–7.

"W-2 Workers Handling Food Stamps Will Move to One Office." 2003. *Milwaukee Journal Sentinel*, 2 May, B3.

5

Privatization, Labor-Management Relations, and Working Conditions for Lower-Skilled Employees

Immanuel Ness and Roland Zullo

What is the effect of privatization on the employment conditions of service workers? Privatization advocates depict upwardly mobile displaced public workers opportunely entering an expanding private service sector (Moore 1999; Savas 2000). Critics, on the other hand, contend that privatization is a political decision that enables firms to boost profits by depressing the wages and benefits of service workers (Kuttner 1997; Zullo 2002). This debate, however, is not only about economic distribution. At issue is a philosophical question over the role of the state in shaping labor markets. Should the state, on the grounds of efficiency, privatize services and thereby subject employees to the institutional and legal environment found in the private labor market, *regardless of the negative effects on worker well-being*? Or, rather, should the state endorse gainful employment, fair conditions, and reasonable expectations for job security, first by promoting high standards within public service, and second by refusing to privatize unless comparable standards are met by private contractors?

While this question can be framed as a choice between the right of a few public workers to enjoy "above market" labor conditions against the right of taxpayers to cost-effective services, such an abstraction ignores the historical role of state policy in shaping employment standards and working conditions in the private sector.[1] Moreover, there remains a vested public interest in ensuring that "labor efficiency" does not translate into harsh forms of exploitation that exacerbate demands on public and private social support systems. In this way, the employment consequences of privatization potentially touch both private sector workers and citizens who finance social welfare programs. Once it is recognized that privatization fails in cases where marginal gains in service efficiency occur at the expense of quality jobs, safeguarding the well-being of public employees by incorporating any projected erosion in working conditions into the privatization decision becomes responsible policy.

Guidance on this issue requires a comprehensive understanding of the changes that take place when services shift from public to private control. Research indicates that most dislocated public workers are rehired by private contractors, are reassigned within government, or manage to secure jobs in the private sector labor market (Dudek and Company 1989; GAO 2001). Although workers' ability to obtain new employment is reassuring, little is known about the quality of their new jobs and, specifically, the changes in working conditions for those public employees who survive the transition to private management. Available evidence is not encouraging. Empirical results indicate that privatization exerts downward pressure on compensation (Chandler 1994; Pack 1989; Pendleton 1999; Stevens 1984), implying that privatized service workers suffer a decline in economic status. Further evidence that privatization is more frequent when labor-management relations are contentious (Chandler and Feuille 1994) suggests that private contracting can be a punitive reply to union demands.

Using ethnographic methods, this chapter explores the effect of privatization on labor-management relations and working conditions in health care settings. Our aim is to contribute to the topic of privatization's impact on work in three ways. First, where most prior research was based on surveys of public managers, our data was collected through semistructured, face-to-face interviews with local Union presidents. Union leaders chosen for this project work alongside the rank-and-file members who elected them. We therefore assume that their statements broadly reflect the experiences of the membership. Second, departing from prior work that tracked displaced public workers, we focus attention on a set of occupations in order to examine conditions for workers who survived the transition to private control, as well as those hired afterward. We specifically target lower-skilled support service positions—housekeeping, laundry, food service, and custodial services—because women, minorities, and immigrants disproportionately fill these jobs. In doing so we hope to contribute to the discussion of privatization's effects on women (Bernhardt and Dresser 2002), minorities (Stein 1994; Suggs 1989), and low-skilled workers (Erickcek, Houseman, and Kalleberg 2002; Mason and Siegel 1997). Third, taking advantage of the face-to-face interview format, we explore the productivity-enhancing methods of private contractors and their effect on a broad range of workplace conditions, such as work stress, job security, and disciplinary policy. We also ask leaders to comment on the quality of client care before and after privatization.

Research Background

The six sites are listed in Table 5.1. All of the health care facilities are located in the vicinity of New York City. Sites were selected to provide variation in privatization policy. At one extreme is a hospital that was fully transferred to private, for-profit interests in 1998 (Site 1). At the other extreme are health centers that remain almost exclusively public (Sites 2 and 3). Between these models are two health centers that remain public, but where management has contracted some support services to for-profit entities. One of these health centers has outsourced patient food services to a private, for-profit firm (Site 4). Another has recently privatized housekeeping, food services, and laundry (Site 5). A sixth hospital was converted to a public benefit corporation in 2001 and has outsourced the laundry to a private contractor (Site 6).

A union represents workers at all sites. Table 5.1 also provides local union size and information on the union president. The union presidents we interviewed have had a wide range of experience and tenure in their positions, ranging from less than one year to twenty years. All negotiated at least one labor agreement. Differences in tenure reflect experience in labor-management relations and knowledge of the effect of privatization policy. The interviews with union leaders lasted from one to two hours. Taped interview data was transcribed, analyzed, and cross-referenced by documents, such as union contracts and organizational correspondence. What follows are the major themes from the union leader interviews.

Union Size, Composition, and Collective
Bargaining Structure

In any collective bargaining context, the balance of power between labor and management is partially a function of the size and composition

Table 5.1

Health Care Sites, Union Size, and Union Leader Characteristics

Site	Organization type	Extent of union privatization	Number of members	Union leader initials	Tenure as union president	Number of contracts negotiated	Years at employer
1	Private, for-profit	Complete	500	A.B.	20	10	30
2	State public	None	390	J.S.	12	4	27
3	County public	None	1,000	W.R.	3	2	31
4	State public	Partial (F)	650	S.K.	6	2	20
5	County public	Partial (F, H, L)	260	R.F.	1	1	6
6	Public benefit corporation	Partial (L)	3,200	G.W.	6	4	26

Key: F = food service; H = housekeeping; L = laundry.

of the union. State statutes that enable public workers to unionize often allow first-line supervisors to form unions, as is the case in New York and New Jersey. Occasionally first-line supervisors and subordinates are in the same bargaining unit. In contrast, private sector law excludes supervisors from coverage. Unionized public supervisors are therefore vulnerable when bargaining shifts to the private sector legal environment, as A.B., union president at Site 1, describes: "That's the first thing they did when they took over. They got rid of the supervisors." A.B. explains how management thinned the ranks by encouraging union members to accept supervisory positions and then firing them: "They came in and they promoted them and then they dumped them. They dumped them, that's what they did." Such tactics undermine the power of the union, first by reducing the overall size of the bargaining unit; second by eliminating senior, influential rank-and-file leaders; and third by creating different, competing interests groups within the workforce.

Another structural factor affecting the balance of power is whether bargaining is atomized or multisite. As public employees, union members benefit from both multisite bargaining and from contemporaneous negotiations at other state or municipal units. G.W., union president at Site 6, expresses concern over the hospital's attempt to separate the bargaining process from the county pattern:

> They want their own bargaining unit to negotiate separate from the county. The way it sits right now, we are one bargaining unit (with the county). So who sits at the table is the union and our members. On the other side of the table sits the public benefit corporation administration and the county administration. But the hospital doesn't want that. So the hospital is going through the process [of separating us from the county] saying that we should be a separate bargaining unit. . . . When we were negotiating with the county, the county may offer a 10 percent cost of living and they [hospital management] say I don't want to.

Management at Site 6, a public benefit corporation, has already demanded an increase in the workweek from thirty-five hours to forty hours and concessions on vacation time. G.W. is acutely aware that his ability to prevent further concessions depends on whether his local is signatory to the broader county agreement.

While bargaining units become smaller and fragmented, union leaders are often required to deal with employers that are national in scope. A.B. describes his frustration negotiating with the new management company, based in Colorado: "I was sitting there listening—but [their negotiator] was just the go-between man . . . he had to get in touch with Colorado before he could accept anything." When negotiators at the bargaining table lack the authority to sign off on contract terms, it generally indicates a failure to bargain in good faith. For our purposes, it illustrates how bargaining moves away from the shop, further from the control of local union leaders.

Changes in the unit composition and bargaining structure create an opportunity for employers to engage in concession or "hard" bargaining. A.B. negotiated one contract with the new private management team and anticipates forthcoming negotiations to be difficult. "Well, right now we have a contract . . . and that contract was like very hard—it was very hard—so I'm looking for the next contract to be even harder the next time around." He notes that in the last contract "we lost fifteen holidays, paid vacations, paid personal leave, birthdays. Now we're down to like eight holidays—we've lost a lot—fifteen sick days a year—we lost that."

In comparison, union leaders in the public sector have avoided concessions. However, this is not, as J.S., the local union president at Site 2, asserts, because labor and management concur on every matter: "I think that there are some years where it is very contentious dealing with certain issues and some years where it's not. You know, I've been on bargaining tables all over with the governor and the negotiators were absolute pigs." Rather, J.S. finds influence through political action: "We send faxes to the governor and while it sometimes goes on very long, you know, ultimately we get decent contracts." Similarly, W.R., local president at Site 3, remarks, "This last bargaining went excellent. Gentle. Our regional unit president negotiates with the county executive for a contract for all county employees. Bargaining here became easier rather than more difficult, due to our legislative activity." Perhaps the most critical source of power that public workers lose through privatization is their ability to exert leverage through the political system.

Unfair Labor Practices and Grievances

A healthy labor-management relationship typically has few grievances and no unfair labor practices. By these measures, relations are significantly more strained in units experiencing privatization. A.B. (Site 1) observes: "When we were run by the county it was more of a family atmosphere with the workers and management, but [after privatization] it's just strictly business." Consequently, says A.B., we are "filing unfair labor practices all the time." Confrontation is routine for vice president E.A. (Site 1): "We look forward to [meeting with managers] every day, because we know what kind of fight we have ahead of us . . . when we leave home in the morning because we don't know what's gonna happen when we get there." As for the rights in the contract, E.A. adds, "We have a union contract, we try to abide by it. The hospital won't abide by it."

According to G.W. (Site 6), "We go in and we try to talk to them and try straightening things out before we do grievances." But in the end, "we go a lot to arbitration with disciplines and grievances . . . and file a lot of unfair labor practices." Much of the conflict arises from a rigid application of rules. Inflexible scheduling, for example, has made it difficult for members to balance work and family obligations.

> In a recent grievance, a single mother complained that management arbitrarily changed her shift so that she was unable to take care of her children when they arrived at home. The woman had no recourse and went home her normal time to care for her children. As a result, she was written up for leaving the job without prior approval. I feel for her because my hands are tied.

G.W. sees the new management style as a function of union animus, rather than a necessity for workplace productivity. The hospital administrator, says G.W., "is not union-friendly—he tolerates us, but he is not union-friendly."

At Site 5, local union president R.F. expresses confidence in his ability to confer with management. Nevertheless, R.F. admits that he has yet to speak to any high-level manager—including management for his very own unit, building services. "I would try to sit and talk to the CEO of the hospital. I will try to get in touch with [the supervisor] of building services." Asked whether managers respond, R.F. replies, "They will—they will—but I haven't got to that point yet."

The grievance procedure at Site 4 is a major source of contention for local union leadership. According to local president S.K., workers frequently are required to follow management orders against their better judgment. If they have a problem with an order, they must follow it and then file a grievance. If they are disciplined, they are presumed guilty until they file a grievance to get the discipline overturned. Grievances are not resolved at a local level, but are ultimately decided by higher-level union officials and top-level management. Since most workers cannot take action on a local level, S.K. says that management is free to violate the contract without repercussions.

Stable union and management leadership has engendered more positive relations in the public sector units. Referring to union grievances, J.S. (Site 2) comments, "I would not say that they are hostile to us. I would say that every year or two a major issue comes up where we really butt heads with them and maintain our antagonistic posture, but we grow with them and they grow with us." The union processes grievances at Site 2 fairly efficiently, and management addresses complaints. J.S. provides an example:

> Four years ago we had a whole struggle around the issue of racism in the area of promotions, so we did a study about it and what the grounds were.... The initiative did not actually come from this office, it came from the people ... who actually work here and we took it on and saw a lot of people promoted as a result, so management did not back away from it.

One factor facilitating dispute resolution is an institutionalized process for sharing information and ideas with management. J.S. says, "We have seminars and meetings with management the last Wednesday of every month, in which we take minutes regularly."

At Site 3, local union president W.R. characterizes "relations with management, most of the time it is fine. We have a good working relationship." W.R. does express dissatisfaction with the recently appointed commissioner of hospitals: "He is pure mean. We have a lot of issues today—cutting overtime and staff." He continues: "The commissioner likes to expand power. We are fighting everything from uniforms to you name it. Every little thing is a fight." However, unlike the private sector, within government there are often multiple centers of authority to which a union can turn to mitigate the effect of an aggressive appointee. During the interview, W.R. described the health department commissioner as such an ally: "Breath of fresh air. She said, 'I will do anything to help workers to be paid appropriately.'"

Job Security and Worker Turnover

The interviews reveal a direct correlation between concessions, aggressive disciplinary action, and declining job security. Soon after the initial transition to private control, private contractors tolerate—even encourage—employee turnover to thin the ranks and sustain a low-wage workforce. At Site 5, local union president R.F. deals with terminations on an ongoing basis. "There was a lot of change, like there were a lot of disciplinary actions. There were like five people, we got like five terminations a week—it was going out of chaos." Some of the terminated workers were never replaced, and there remain roughly 250 to 275 workers employed in housekeeping and laundry services, down from 500 before the management change. Many workers voluntarily quit in response to the concessions, explains R.F.: "Only twenty workers remain from among 260 seven years ago—when the country privatized the hospital and significantly reduced wages and benefits." When Site 5 privatized housekeeping and laundry, wages were slashed by more than 50 percent from about $18 an hour to $8 an hour. R.F. offers a blunt assessment: "Well, pay—salary—it's no good here, there's no benefits, no pension. [Workers] were better off with the county." Concessions and harsh disciplinary action induce rapid turnover, purging the organization of workers who expect to earn living wages and benefits.

Site 5 is not an isolated case. A.B., local union president at Site 1, describes a systematic program by private management to eliminate senior employees: "See what happened was they laid off everybody in the dietary section, and kept some of the ones [that were] here for six months, or eight months. Then they privatized the dietary department." Moreover, antagonistic disciplinary policy discourages union members from seeking relief through the grievance process. According to A.B., "sometimes workers are so intimidated by management that they fail to file grievances when they are terminated."

Circumventing contractual seniority provisions to either downsize or rid the organization of senior employees was a consistent theme. President G.W. describes the dismissal strategy at Site 6 when the laundry was closed:

> They [management] put them [laundry workers] in departments. And because they had to go into a new department they're suppose to be doing their probation again, so they had six months' probation. I tried to get that away, but they [management] wouldn't do that. Then four months later they [management] come up with layoffs and now these people are in the middle of layoffs.

The closure of the laundry led to significant job cuts in the hospital. G.W. describes the effect on employment: "Since January of 2002, man-

agement has cut 360 some odd workers, reducing the union membership from about 3,500 employees—now we're down to 3,200. The majority of the cuts came from closing the laundry."

Job insecurity, a direct and intentional outcome of a competitive bidding policy, does not spare management personnel. President G.W. (Site
6) says, "Well, in the past six years I have seen four administrators,"
explaining, "We had Marriott here, we had Owens Healthcare, and they
both are no longer here." At Site 1, private management acted swiftly
once it had authority to manage. A.B. comments: "They terminate the
workers, they terminate the managers—seems like they don't have any
respect."

Part-Time Labor, Client Labor, and Workloads

One significant change under privatization is an accelerated use of contingent and part-time workers, who typically receive lower pay and
fewer benefits. At Site 1, management is increasingly hiring temporary
workers to reduce overtime, an issue that creates tension with the union.
Union president A.B. observes that "the number of workers have declined because of part-timers. . . . We didn't have no part-timers when
they first took over." Prior to privatization, "we had 149 full-time workers
in environmental . . . includ(ing) supervisors and we had more than 100
in dietary—say, 275 between the two." Under public management, the
use of part-time workers was limited to "the weekend—just Saturday
to Sunday." Under private management, "every time there is a termina-
tion or someone quit, that's what they do, they make two positions out
of it." By doing so, management does not have to pay health benefits to
the workers.

Union leaders at Site 6 voice similar complaints. When the new management took over, full-time workers essentially lost their rights to overtime, a source of income workers depend on. According to President
G.W., "If we are short on housekeepers, nonunion independent contractors would be hired, performing the same tasks as union workers." G.W.
asserts that the hospital is "in the process of . . . replacing the full-time
employees with temp workers." This eliminates union positions.

At Site 2, the use of part-time employees has increased sharply in the
last two years. Union president J.S. attributes the rise in part-timers to
state budget cuts and hiring freezes. He notes, however, that part-time
workers scheduled for at least twenty hours a week are entitled to the

same rights and benefits as full-time workers. This provision acts to ensure against the loss of full-time jobs. Moreover, J.S. points out that contract language mandates that part-timers working more than twenty hours be paid overtime, or "what's called extra time—which is that time between 20 hours and 40 hours . . . so it's like overtime in the same way that full-timers are paid overtime." Overtime is also a way of *not* hiring more workers. Laying off workers and giving overtime to the remaining workers is hardly a good thing for the union, even if some workers benefit.

At Site 4, patients are replacing full-time workers. Since 1999, management has, ostensibly as a form of therapy, required patients to perform groundskeeping duties without compensation. Patients working in the food services department are paid $5 an hour. Union president S.K. questions the expediency of this policy:

> They are not trained for some of the jobs that they are doing and some of the jobs they are doing require training on sanitary techniques, which is not a part of their therapeutic atmosphere right now. I mean, to become a food service worker in New York State is competitive. You have to take a test and there are also other things involved with that. These people are not trained and they push them to do the work.

S.K. estimates that about one-quarter of the facility's 400 patients are in the work program. In his opinion, the primary purpose is not to educate patients, but rather, "It is to cut costs by any means necessary. It is to cut cost and not pay for labor." When he demanded information, S.K. was denied the list of temporary employers and employees from management. "They claimed that it was the privacy of the employees; that I don't get that information. . . . They work for a private company and I told management that it was affecting my membership."

Reductions in full-time staff, coupled with the use of inexperienced part-time contingent and client labor, has intensified the workload for the remaining full-time employees. Commenting on his members, President R.F. (Site 5) notes, "These workers work their butt off. They do their work, they are respectable, intelligent, they know how to deal with people, you know." He adds, "[workers] got more ground to cover now than before." President G.W. at Site 6 echoes this sentiment:

> The layoffs have left a lot of the departments so shorthanded people are just overworked. Management will not hire the staff that they need, and

that is what I am constantly dealing with day in and day out. They will not replace, and if they do go in and replace somebody, they put a contractor or a temporary worker in, and then we go and we fight and they take them away.

G.W. observes that staffing shortages are not limited to his members: "We can't get OR nurses, we can't get ER nurses—[the hospital doesn't] pay enough money for them, which reduces the number of patients and revenue for the hospital."

Quality and Content of Service

Pressures to cut costs have negative consequences for patients. Service conditions have significantly eroded under private management at Site 1, a main health care provider in northern New Jersey. Union president A.B. observes that after privatization, "a lot of stuff was going on, . . . Management was trying to cut the length of time patients were staying so they had a great big meeting . . . and started scrutinizing our people to keep an eye on them." At the operational level, union leaders are required to fight for the basic upkeep of sanitation equipment. A.B. provides an example: "Right now the dishwashing machine been down about three or four months, and we've been going to top management concerning [this issue]. We're gonna probably have to end up doing some kind of demonstration or something to make them move." The decline in basic service is widespread, as A.B., notes: "You know the quality of the food, you just know they don't get quality food . . . cheaper food." Vice President E.A. adds, "They buy, you know, the plastic forks and they break before you can eat the food."

Likewise, at Site 4, a facility that provides services to about 400 patients, New York State outsourced food services to Sysco Systems, a private supplier and distributor of prepackaged food. Prior to 1999, food was prepared on-site by qualified public workers. Now the food is packaged at an off-site facility, trucked into the center, and heated for serving. As a result, union president S.K. estimates that his local lost about 100 of the union's 750 jobs, mostly through attrition.

Pressure at Site 6 is producing similar effect on services. Says G.W., "[management has] eliminated the Center for Primary Care for patients who can't afford a private doctor." In addition, G.W. notes that the new managers have closed the laundry, "which limits the availability of clean bed sheets, towels, etc. They've eliminated poison control, and we now have a private ambulance corporation." Union leaders, such as G.W., acknowledge that contracting can reduce costs. However, they also point out that significant savings can usually be traced to erosion in patient services. The following statement by G.W. is illustrative:

> When we did laundry our laundry was up on the floor every day. Every day we were up there, and put sheets, and all other clean laundry. But this new contractor that comes in is doing them every three days. They are changing the sheets every three days. When the new contractor came, they said they can save you money and that's what [the hospital's chief executive officer] was looking for, to save money. They proved it in black and white that if they closed the laundry up that we will save $1.5 million, because the laundry cost $3 million to run a year.

In this case, the cost of laundry services was halved, but only by reducing the level of services by approximately two-thirds. From the union perspective, such large-scale reductions in service contribute to declining patient enrollment, exacerbating the hospital's financial difficulties. G.W. explains that Site 6 was, until recently, "the best hospital that you can go to, but we just don't have the clientele anymore to do that. I mean, the workers here, they work very hard; they are very good; they are good at what they do; they are professional, and they are loyal— but there ain't many of us. They broke down the workforce so it's getting less and less and less."

Union leaders are sensitive to the limits to cutbacks and to the importance of a stable workforce for patient rehabilitation. S.K., at Site 4 elaborates:

> Because when you work here, you work in a place like this you become attached, you know? I mean you become attached emotionally, psychologically, you understand? And then in a lot of aspects you get yourself involved. You know the clients themselves. They become a part of you. If I walk in that building right now, all the patients know me. They become part of my family.

President J.S., at Site 2, offered a succinct comment on the relationship between workforce cutbacks and client care: "You need to be in human contact to help people get better."

Moreover, J.S. emphasizes the importance of bargaining as equals with management to arrive at policy that improves conditions for workers and patients. One example involved the use of precautions and restraints for patients who become violent and pose a risk to themselves and workers. J.S. circulated a petition to members, gathered ideas, and presented a proposal to management. Ultimately, says J.S., "We negotiated a very strict protocol for the use of restraints." Describing the negotiations, J.S. concludes, "we backed them off another policy and came to a pretty good place."

Conclusion and Discussion

Who should define the benchmark for labor relations and working conditions in the service sector, government or the private market? Fundamentally, deciding whether government should factor the fate of displaced public workers into the privatization decision is to ask whether service workers deserve a significant role in shaping the terms of employment. As this testimony indicates, public employment provides service workers with a broader range of institutional levers for securing gainful employment, fair conditions, and quality services. The levers exist at two levels. First, most public workers enjoy civil service rules that protect against capricious standards for promotions and job assignments and offer due process. Second, when workers are unionized, the public sector collective bargaining context is more favorable, on both legal and political terms, providing union leaders with power to negotiate and enforce contract terms. On most occasions, especially for lower-skilled service workers, privatization disables these institutional levers, shifting power to employers. If allowed, private employers respond by extracting concessions. In some instances, compensation and working conditions deteriorate to where private contractors have difficulty attracting qualified employees. Yet government leaders do have the option of establishing basic standards as a condition for privatization. When that happens, societal norms and expectations, as expressed through democratic institutions, such as labor unions, good faith negotiations, and the electoral process, shape labor and employment conditions.

Generally, responses by local union leaders expose stark differences in wages, benefits, working conditions, and patient care across public and privatized institutions. Consistently, where privatization has been applied, union leaders lament that management wields power capriciously and arbitrarily and that union capacity to bargain effectively and to represent workers is weakened and compromised. In all privatized units, union leaders note that significant concessions have been made—wage reductions, elimination of health benefits, cutbacks in sick days and vacation days, and so forth. In health centers that have not been privatized, union leaders acknowledge differences with management. However, these differences are bridged through good-faith negotiations in a labor-management relationship that union leaders characterize as one with mutual respect. By and large, where private contracting is absent, union leaders have been able to sustain more favorable wages, benefits, and working conditions.

Statements by these union leaders are consistent with theory: post-privatization internal labor market restructuring increases labor "efficiency." Yet with the possible exception of food service, very little improvement occurs through new technology or organizational design. Rather, labor efficiency was achieved at the expense of service workers and, to some extent, the quality and quantity of client services. This does not imply that *all* workers are harmed by privatization. Private contractors commonly recruit key personnel from former public services to manage privatized operations, resulting in status and compensation upgrades for *some* displaced public employees. However, in our examples such offers were rare. When offers did extend to lesser-skilled public workers, testimony indicates that the aim was to lure workers away from the protective seniority provisions in the labor agreement and then terminate them. Given that the workforce was composed predominantly of people of color, women, and immigrants, these changes in job security and work quality disproportionately harm protected groups who have historically depended on the public sector for economic opportunities.

Union leaders identify three primary methods for enhancing labor efficiency: wage and benefit concessions, work intensification, and part-time and contingent labor. While previous research focused on wages, union members in our study more often experienced a decline in benefits that accrue with tenure, such as vacations and sick days. Targeting benefits that are linked to employment longevity is consistent with a strategy of pressuring senior workers to exit. Work intensification, which is achieved primarily by downsizing staff, also disproportionately affects older workers. Concessions plus heavier workloads amount to a crude formula for eliminating full-time regular employees. As the testimony indicates, when private companies do replace senior workers, they prefer to backfill with lower-cost, part-time, contingent, and even client replacements. Union leaders testify that this staff restructuring strategy is partially responsible for the decline in service quality and quantity.

Finally, we note an interaction between privatization, perceived union instrumentality, and union strategy. As described, a reduction in bargaining power manifests as wage and benefit concessions, heavier workloads, inflexible scheduling, less grievance protection, and so forth. Union leaders commented that members frequently do not connect these outcomes to privatization policy, instead directing their dissatisfaction toward the union. Clearly some members who suffer a dramatic decline in job quality quit. Members who remain, however, respond by demanding new union leadership. Our examples indicate that union leaders who retain their positions during the privatization transition are pushed into a more radical mode. Two of the union leaders we interviewed were experienced negotiators who decided to confront private management. A second observable outcome is for experienced leaders to step down. A union leader in one privatized institution had never negotiated a contract when the institution was controlled and run by the county. In such cases, survival of the local may depend on whether leadership turnover signifies a rejuvenation process for rebuilding union power.

Notes

This research was sponsored by Poverty and Race Research Action Council (PRRAC), a Washington, D.C.–based organization dedicated to improving the quality of life among people of color, women, and immigrants residing in the United States. Supplemental financial support was received from the City University of New York Diversity Grants Program and the University of Michigan Graduate School.

1. Examples include labor and employment legislation. Recently, the local "living-wage" movement seeks to lift the wages and benefits of workers in the private sector by requiring wage and benefit minimums as a condition for public contracts (Nissen 1998; Pollin and Luce 1998).

References

Bernhardt, Annette, and Laura Dresser. 2002. "Why Privatizing Government Services Would Hurt Women Workers." Washington DC: Center for Women's Policy Research.
Chandler, Timothy D. 1994. "Sanitation Privatization and Sanitation Employees Wages." *Journal of Labor Research* 15, no. 2 (Spring): 137–53.

Chandler, Timothy D., and Peter Feuille. 1994. "Cities, Unions, and the Privatization of Sanitation Services." *Journal of Labor Research* 15, no. 1 (Winter): 53–71.

Dudek and Company. 1989. *The Long Term Employment Implications of Privatization: Evidence from Selected U.S. Cities and Counties*. Prepared for the Nation Commission for Employment Policy, Report No. 98–04, March.

Erickcek, George, Susan Houseman, and Arne Kalleberg. 2002. "The Effects of Temporary Services and Contracting Out on Low Skilled Workers: Evidence from Auto Suppliers, Hospitals and Public Schools." Upjohn Institute Staff Working Paper No. 03–90. Kalamazoo, MI: Upjohn Institute.

GAO (General Accounting Office). 2001. *DOD Competitive Sourcing: Effects of A-76 Studies on Federal Employees' Employment, Pay and Benefits Vary*. Washington, DC: General Accounting Office, GAO-01–388, March.

Kuttner, Robert. 1997. *Everything for Sale: The Virtues and Limits of Markets*. New York: Alfred A. Knopf.

Mason, Maryann, and Wendy Siegel. 1997. *Does Privatization Pay? A Case Study of Privatization in Chicago*. Chicago: Chicago Institute on Urban Poverty, January.

Moore, Stephen. 1999. "How Contracting Out City Services Impacts Public Employees." In *Contracting Out Government Services*, ed. Paul Seidenstat, pp. 211–18. Westport, CT: Praeger.

Nissen, Bruce. 1998. "The Impact of a Living Wage Ordinance on Miami-Dade County." Miami: Center for Labor Research and Studies, Florida International University.

Pack, Janet Rothenberg. 1989. "Privatization and Cost Reduction." *Policy Sciences* 22, no. 1 (February): 1–25.

Pendleton, Andrew. 1999. "Ownership or Competition? An Evaluation of the Effects of Privatization on Industrial Relations Institutions, Processes and Outcomes." *Public Administration* 77, no. 4: 769–91.

Pollin, Robert, and Stephanie Luce. 1998. *The Living Wage: Building a Fair Economy*. New York: New Press.

Savas, Emanuel S. 2000. *Privatization and Public-Private Partnerships*. New York: Chatham House Publishers.

Stein, Lana. 1994. "Privatization, Workforce Cutbacks, and African American Municipal Employment." *American Review of Public Administration* 24, no. 2 (June): 181–91.

Stevens, Barbara J. 1984. *Delivering Municipal Services Efficiently: A Comparison of Municipal and Private Service Delivery*. Washington, DC: U.S. Department of Housing and Urban Development.

Suggs, Robert E. 1989. *Minorities and Privatization: Economic Mobility at Risk*. Washington, DC: Joint Center for Political Studies (distributed by University Press of America, Lanham, MD).

Zullo, Roland. 2002. "Confronting the Wicked Witch and Exposing the Wizard: Public Sector Unions and Privatization Policy." *Working USA* 6, no. 2 (Fall): 9–39.

6

The Workforce Investment Act and the Labor Movement

Helena Worthen

Some assertions seem so obvious that it is embarrassing to state them explicitly. We know that the following are true: minimum wage or near-minimum wage jobs do not pay enough to keep people out of poverty; parents who work at low-wage jobs and try to go to school at the same time find it impossible to spend enough time with their children; children who grow up in poverty and who have little contact with overworked, exhausted adults stand little chance of taking advantage of school and community resources that may help them break out of poverty; union jobs pay better than non-union jobs; and training does not increase the likelihood of someone getting a union job—organizing a union is what does that.

Yet the arguments that are being made today about how this country should deal with the swelling ranks of the poor, the loss of good jobs, and the failures of our educational system are being framed in terms laid out by two pieces of legislation, the Personal Responsibility and Work Opportunity Reconciliation Act of 1996 (PRWORA, also referred to as "welfare reform" or TANF, Temporary Assistance to Needy Families) and the Workforce Investment Act of 1998 (WIA), which do not acknowledge these truths. Under TANF, work is offered as the answer to poverty, but it is work that earns below-poverty-level wages. Under WIA, training is the answer to both the loss of jobs and the failures of our educational system, but it is only short-term training for locally specified "growth" industries, and even this only for the lucky few. The idea that training is what pulls people out of poverty (that high-skill jobs inevitably are high-wage jobs) is so deeply buried in our national ideology that the U.S. Department of Labor's 200-page 1999 *Report on the American Workforce* explains that in its statistical analysis it used wages as a proxy for skills: "Relative wages are used as a measure of relative skill assuming that wages, on average, reflect the value of a worker's production. Workers who earn more are assumed to have higher under-lying skills" (46).

When this assumption and its corollaries about the labor market are put into practice, they give us a national employment training policy that is at worst punitive, at best a Band-Aid. Yet WIA, at least, came about through a desire to fix what appeared to be the key problems with previous national employment policies. How these efforts collapsed into an overall system that pushes desperate people into bad jobs, keeps wages low, and subsidizes a workforce that appears to be mostly below the radar of the labor movement is a story worth retelling.

WIA as the Most Recent Phase of the Job Creation Versus Job Training Cycle

The big distinction between employment policies is between those that create jobs and those that do not. Explicit government involve-ment in employment policy goes back at least to the Depression, with the Works Progress Administration (WPA) in 1935. Under the WPA, public policy was to create jobs. Training was secondary to employment. Public projects were created and people were hired to do the work. The people hired were then trained if necessary. The quality of some entry-level training jobs was regulated: in 1937 the Fitzgerald Act set up a registration system to monitor the quality of apprenticeship programs and oversee the welfare of apprentices (a model unfortunately not copied by WIA). With the Cold War, policy turned from job creation to training. We saw the creation of the Of-fice of Manpower, the Vocational Education Act, and the JOBS pro-gram, none of which created jobs; the idea was that if we train people, jobs will come. During the 1970s the Comprehensive Employment and Training Act (CETA) did create public sector jobs, some of which involved training. Margaret Weir, the Berkeley sociologist, describes these policy shifts back and forth between job creation (or even full employment) and job training as a continuing debate that began in the 1940s and entered its final stages in the late 1970s (Weir 1992, 131). When CETA became a target of criticisms of government waste and interference in the labor market, it was replaced by the Job Training Partnership Act (JTPA) in 1982, a training, not a job creation act, which then became our primary federal employment training program until WIA was implemented in 2000.

But "primary" does not mean "only." JTPA was only one of over a hundred programs. When the General Accounting Office (GAO) reviewed federal programs related to employment and training in 1994, it found 154 programs run by 14 federal agencies spending $25 billion per year (GAO 1994). Many programs were redundant but each had its own targeted populations, reporting requirements, services, and often proprietary information systems. The GAO summarized its findings this way:

> Past efforts to fix the system have fallen short. As a result, more programs evolve every year and the problems inherent in the system loom even larger. GAO testified that a major structural overhaul and consolidation of employment training programs is needed. (GAO 1994).

Meanwhile, in 1993 the Department of Labor had already set up a working group to prepare a report (*The Employment Services Revitalization Work Plan*, which came out in October 1994) that would include many features later incorporated into WIA: the concept of universal access; use of One-Stop offices; the three-tier triage approach, consisting of core (quick assessment and referral to jobs), intensive (longer but still brief programs involving some staff intervention), and training services; and upgrading of job-matching information systems (Fay and Lippoldt 1999, 1981). The Department of Labor then announced a competitive grant program to set up One-Stop centers; by 1998, about 800 One-Stop centers were in operation (86). These would become models for expansion of the system.

However, in the partisan atmosphere after the 1994 midterm election, welfare reform, the hot button issue of the conservatives, had to come first. Any support for training now had to be linked to pushing people into the workforce. So PRWORA was signed in 1996 by President Clinton, putting a five-year lifetime cap on the span of an individual's welfare benefits, and welfare gave way to welfare-to-work. This cleared the way for WIA.

At the Rose Garden signing ceremony, President Clinton remarked that WIA was an answer to his dream of consolidating this blizzard of government programs into one grant that we could give a person who was unemployed or under-employed so that they could decide. . . what to do with the help we were giving them on the theory that they would know what is in their own best interest and be able to pursue it. (White House 1998)

The media spin on WIA was that it would create opportunities for workers to exercise individual choice. The Associated Press (1998) wrote: "Out-of-work Americans will be able to buy job-training services under a 'GI Bill' for workers that President Clinton signed Friday." The *Cincinnati Enquirer* published an editorial referring again to this "GI Bill of sorts," saying that WIA

dissolves important government training programs that devour $8 to $10 billion a year without providing much of a benefit to workers and employers. . . . Best of all, for individuals, vouchers will enable them to shop around for what they need. . . . The biggest winners are workers. ("Good Job" 1998)

In the Senate, Paul Wellstone, Democrat of Minnesota, and Mike DeWine, Republican of Ohio, were WIA's cosponsors. Wellstone was reported as saying, "It's a good piece of work" (Broder 1998). But Mike DeWine pointed out another problem that WIA was intended to solve before resolving issues of redundancy of programs. A reporter for the *Dayton Daily News* quoted him as saying, "This is the unfinished business of welfare reform. We had not given [welfare recipients] one of the tools they really needed to make welfare reform work" (Joyce 1998).

At the time WIA was signed, the unemployment rate was declining from a twelve-year high of 7.5 percent in 1996 to a thirty-year low of 4.5 percent (U.S. Department of Labor 1999, 135). When the labor market is tight and upward pressure on wages is developing, a cogent argument in favor of funding for training is that training can increase productivity without increasing wages. Since WIA funding is also available to employers on a contract basis to train incumbent employees, it was not just a GI Bill for workers; it was also a way to subsidize in-house training.

So WIA became the vehicle for doing four things at once—rationalizing our federal and state workforce development systems (as part of the "reinventing government" cuts); giving workers a GI Bill–type "choice"; providing a mechanism for moving people coming off wel-

fare into work; and providing employers with training options that would
alleviate the high-skill labor shortage that was part of the boom economy
of the 1990s. No one piece of legislation could successfully do these
mutually contradictory things.

After it was signed in August 1998, WIA dropped from the public
view. States began the two-year planning period that would lead up to
implementation in July 2000. By June 1999, the AFL-CIO's Working
for America Institute had put out a fine handbook for labor movement
people who would become involved in WIA implementation, but it was
not widely disseminated. During the planning period, service dropped
drastically. According to the *Employment and Training Reporter* (2003a),
"the number of individuals trained during the transfer to WIA
represent[ed] 25% of the total for the last year of JTPA" (501). But
unemployment was low and continuing to drop, so the lack of service
did not matter much to most working people. And at a time when the
arrival of a new employer in town would start a bidding war as employees jumped ship for better-paying jobs, who would have imagined that
the boom would not last forever?

What WIA Is Not

As a consolidation bill that tidies up what was viewed as a bureaucratic
nightmare, it is important to understand what WIA is not. Unlike other
employment-related legislation, it does not establish a right and then set
up an agency that enforces that right. This makes it different from, for
example, the National Labor Relations Act, which established the right
of workers to form unions and set up the National Labor Relations Board,
and from Title VII of the Civil Rights Act of 1964, which established the
right to a workplace free from various kinds of discrimination and set
up the Equal Employment Opportunity Commission to enforce it. Thus,
although WIA is about training for jobs, there is nothing in WIA that
says that people have the right to enough training, literacy, or vocational
rehabilitation to make them employable or that, once employable, they
have the right to a job. Although WIA is supposed to be about education,
it does not add support to our existing educational institutions. It does
not put money into vocational or technical high schools. Instead, WIA
simply links up mostly existing programs and creates the bureaucracy
that can administer them.

Nor is WIA a fully funded tertiary education system. While it is a channel for funding, the funds that flow through it are a creation of the political process and may be augmented or disappear. For example, WIA was funded at just over $3.5 billion for 2001, according to Federal Funds Information for States (FFIS 2001). This is not a lot of money: it is nearly a billion less, for example, than JTPA got in 1998, the year WIA was signed. By way of contrast, the National Governors Association (NGA) estimates that "in recent years, American businesses have spent more than $232 billion annually on workforce training" (NGA 1997). Our food stamp program alone was funded at $20 billion for 2001 (FFIS 2001). So WIA in 2001 was federally funded at a level which makes it look like a pilot program, not like a system intended to serve the entire U.S. labor force, which was 132.4 million in 1996 (U.S. Department of Labor 1999, 49). However, funding for workforce development does come into WIA through other federal, state, and local funding streams, such as adult education, vocational education, vocational rehabilitation, and economic and community development programs, so the total, although still low, can be slightly augmented from these other sources. But at this level of funding, if no WIA funds at all were spent on administration, there would be $132 available for each currently employed worker to spend on vouchers once every five years.

Most important for our purposes, WIA was never a project of organized labor. Despite the fact that WIA focuses on the entry of people into work, the designers of WIA did not make organized labor a partner (as compared to Canada, where sectoral business-labor training programs were established; see Gunderson and Sharpe 1998). Nor was organized labor effectively able to insist on playing a central role. Registered labor-management apprenticeship programs, for example, which are the most finely tuned examples of successful workforce development programs, stayed away and still stay away from WIA. They get their funding from unions and signatory employer associations; they do not need or want the uncertainties of government funding. Other unions have their own technical training programs (as well as union education). The Working for America Institute of the AFL-CIO stood out in that it committed itself to developing a highly visible set of "high-road" partnerships involving unions, employers, and training, but these were a contrast to, never a part of, WIA implementation.

Cutting out labor was not just an oversight. Key to understanding organized labor's relationship to training is that training the future workforce means organizing the future work. For the building trades

unions in particular, which have the most highly developed training programs, the link between training and organizing is explicit. The commitment to train people is the commitment to organize work for them.
WIA, on the other hand, explicitly states that "Each recipient of funds
under this title shall provide to the Secretary assurances that none of
such funds will be used to assist, promote or deter union organizing"
(Workforce Investment Act, Section 181(b) 782).

WIA's Effect on Labor

Yet despite being virtually excluded from WIA, organized labor is impacted by WIA in four ways. Overall, because it supports training, WIA
engages with one of the concerns of organized labor, which is the future
workforce. Second, by carving out its own universe of training programs,
WIA controls what people will learn in those programs, which in practice means that they will not learn that they have a right to organize and
join a union. WIA thus adds to the critical mass of workers who do not
understand their basic rights in the workplace. Third, although the language of the act says that WIA funds will not be used to "assist, promote, or deter" union organizing, it is by no means a neutrality agreement.
Under the cover of not "promoting" union organizing, practices that
amount to union avoidance take place. Fourth, WIA allows for representative*s* of labor, plural, which is understood to mean at least two, on
workforce investment boards (WIBs), which may have fifty or sixty
members. This minimal level of representation creates a dilemma for
labor representatives. Labor appointees to WIBs ask, "Why, when there
are fifty people on a WIB and there are only two labor people, should I
even bother to go? My vote will mean nothing."

Yet the labor representatives on WIBs have significant, probably un-
realistic oversight and reporting responsibilities. These responsibilities
are evident in the WIA Final Rules (U.S. Department of Labor 2000).

During the WIA comment period, ending in August 2000 with the
publication of the final regulations, many opinions were received from
the field that show up as either accepted or rejected in the final regulations. The Public Policy Department of the AFL-CIO coordinated the
comments from labor organizations and made sure that they were trans-
mitted to the Department of Labor. According to Jane McDonald-Pines
of the AFL-CIO (Jane McDonald-Pines to Helena Worthen, personal
communication, December 6, 2000), virtually all comments and sug-

gestions from labor were rejected. When the AFL-CIO asked why the rejection rate of its comments was so high, the Department of Labor response was that the intent of the law was to devolve maximum discretion to state and local control. The agency explained that labor's suggestions would "limit state and local control" and that they were constrained by the legislation. Yet in reality, given the requirement that 51 percent of the members of WIBs were to be employers or employers' representatives, "local control" meant that employers exercise most of the power at the state and local level. If labor organizations questioned this arrangement, it was construed as attempting to limit this "local control," which the Department of Labor would not consent to.

Nonetheless, in the agency comments printed in the *Federal Register*, the Department of Labor argued that labor representatives on a local WIB were in a good position to take up matters that they took issue with. For example, when one commentator suggested that "State and local boards should be prohibited from developing dislocated worker definitions that exclude groups of workers based on their industry, occupation, or union affiliation," the agency, although agreeing that "workers should not be prohibited from receiving services based on their union affiliation," added that "the union representatives as well as other members of the Local Board have an opportunity to raise concerns regarding consideration of such blanket eligibility decisions" (U.S. Department of Labor 2000, 49314). Time and again, in the final regulations, labor representatives are reminded that they have the opportunity, and are effectively handed the responsibility, for raising concerns that can be broadly depicted as concerning all matters of fairness in the workplace. On a WIB with fifty, sixty, or more participants, this presents a challenge for the two labor representatives.

The kinds of decisions mentioned in the final regulations that are going to be left up to local WIBs and that labor representatives "have an opportunity" to influence include the following:

- What kind of entity should operate a One-Stop? These can be state agencies, nonprofits, educational institutions such as community colleges, or for-profits.
- What mix and duration of services should be offered at a One-Stop? Should training programs include an overview of U.S. labor and employment laws, including Fair Labor Standards Act (FLSA), Occupational Safety and Health Act (OSHA), Family and Medical

Leave Act (FMLA), Americans with Disabilities Act (ADA), and even the National Labor Relations Act (NLRA)?

- What should be the definition of "self-sufficiency" for the purpose of describing the kind of wages a job pays?
- What kind of process constitutes an effective grievance process for WIA participant, provider, vendor, or One-Stop operator or other person or entity? A process that is nothing more than a way to lodge a complaint, and that does not provide for advocacy will not satisfy someone familiar with union grievance processes; neither will a grievance process that sets no precedents or provides no collective benefits.
- What is the appropriate definition of "substantial layoff" and "plant closing"? For example, when there is general public knowledge that a plant is going to close, can the workers at that point be considered "dislocated workers," or do they have to wait until the employer announces the plant closing?
- Should the appropriate labor organization be consulted if a One-Stop program is being considered in which participants will learn skills that are used by an organized trade? A labor representative will answer yes, and that consultation has to happen in advance of action and that the action has to show evidence of the consultation.
- Should a WIB approve contracts with for-profit companies that offer unpaid work experience? Workers engaged in "unpaid work experience" training are not covered by the FLSA. They may not necessarily receive minimum wage or overtime pay or be allowed rest breaks or benefit from other FLSA work standards. What sort of policies covering this situation should be developed?

These questions are all about processes and definitions involved in setting up the WIA system. There are other issues that WIBs (and labor representatives on WIBs) have to deal with once the system is set up. For example: When a training provider is going to be recertified, the criterion of most interest to the WIB is supposed to be the provider's record on job placement. But the labor representative will want to know more. Does the training provider just cream off the best applicants to make its placement numbers look high? If people are being placed in an unpaid work experience situation as part of their "intensive" phase of placement, are they learning anything? What is the "place" where the worker is placed like? Is everyone working mandatory overtime there? Is there a union? What are the workers' benefits? Will the result of the training be a higher-skilled worker who is getting the same pay as before? Is a young, inexpensive worker being trained to take the place of an older, more expensive worker? These questions also apply when WIBs award contracts to train incumbent workers.

As the Working for America Institute (1999) puts it, "The labor representative can be not only an advocate for labor, but also for taxpayers and commonsense fiscal policy." But the answers to questions like these are hard to get and easy to falsify. This is a big assignment for two out of fifty voices at the table.

The Worker as Isolated Consumer of Training

The absence of anything like an introduction to workers' federal legal protections, beginning with the NLRA and including the FLSA, up through the OSHA and the FMLA, is indicative of how a job-seeker is viewed through the lens of the devisers of WIA. All of these legal protections take workers as part of a class, a group of people who can act collectively or, in the language of the NLRA, engage in "concerted activity." In WIA, nothing that suggests that workers engage in the "concerted activity" that is the basis of the NLRA concept of protected activity is mentioned. Instead, WIA envisions the job seeker as an isolated individual, a consumer of training, positioned alone in front of a computer to shop for job or training programs, or managed as a "case" by a caseworker. This is the same mind-set that envisions workers as consumers of goods rather than producers of goods. That only producers who get decent paychecks can become substantial consumers is not part of this calculation.

If the job seeker is isolated, manipulated away from the possibility of collective, concerted activity, the employer is the opposite. By stark contrast, the WIB superstructure of WIA consists of associations of the owners of businesses, established specifically to make common cause with each other.

We have some old, strong language in our labor laws that speaks to this inequity. In 1932, three years before the NLRA was passed, the Norris-LaGuardia Anti-Injunction Act tried to level the playing field between labor and capital somewhat. Section 102 sets out its argument this way:

Whereas under prevailing economic conditions, developed with the aid of governmental authority for owners of property to organize in the corporate and other forms of ownership association, the individual unorganized worker is commonly helpless to exercise actual liberty of contract and to protect his freedom of labor, and thereby to obtain acceptable terms and conditions of employment. (Schwartz 1999, 1)

This is exactly the position WIA puts job seekers in. Employers and representatives of business—"owners of property," as Norris-LaGuardia puts it—are organized into WIBs (a form of ownership association) and make nearly all the decisions, while the job seeker gets case management, not representation. A job seeker coming into a One-Stop, especially someone whose TANF benefits are running out, is "helpless to exercise actual liberty of contract" in exactly this way.

Looking Ahead

An employment policy that is not a shame and a scandal cannot fit into the narrow choices offered by TANF and WIA. Employment policy must encompass trade policy that keeps good jobs at home, raises the minimum wage, provides stipends for families with young children, strengthens our public education system, increases unionization, and provides that some of the value produced by greater worker skills and new technology should go to the workers.

But the wisdom that can put forward the arguments that need to be made in this direction lies in the labor movement, and the labor movement gets called in too late. The labor movement takes on the role of emergency medical technicians (EMTs) who have to save the patient while the ambulance is racing toward the hospital. For example, now that the economy is in trouble, we hear more and more about WIBs partnering with local central labor councils to design training, to study "skill gaps," to set up preapprenticeship programs. Central labor councils become a One-Stop partner in a consortium with community colleges. When plants are closing, Rapid Response teams, funded by state AFL-CIOs, work with laid-off workers to help them through the One-Stop process. After all, who can do it better? Who has the know-how, the relationships, and the trust necessary to do it right? Union-linked training programs have great placement records. But better that the EMTs had been called in before the crisis, to identify unsafe conditions and prevent the accidents—better that the labor movement had been there when the basic structure of our employment policy was being laid out.

This is not to say that the fight to keep funding flowing through WIA or the fight to lift the caps on training under TANF should be abandoned or diverted, nor that the good people who work in the One-Stops trying to get training and job placements for clients should turn out the lights and go home. On the contrary, these are the people who have their fingers in the dikes, who are operating the emergency equipment. But it is dismaying that the battle is being fought on their territory, not on the territory of the labor movement. It is dismaying to see how far what we are defending is from what we need. For example, it is heart-wrenching to see testimony like that of Barbara Gault, director of research for the Institute for Women's Policy Research, speaking before the House Education and the Workforce Committee on March 12, 2002, in which she musters arguments connecting low skills, poor jobs, the need for education, and the importance of improving home life for children, all in the service of pleading that the restrictions on education and training for welfare recipients that are part of TANF can be removed, so that these people can access WIA funding. She is compelled to make an argument from efficiency—"for WIA to realize its full potential"—instead of just saying directly that the direction in which WIA and TANF are converging is wrong (Gault 2002).

The problems that are implicit WIA and TANF are problems of good jobs, good working conditions, and good pay—problems that are rightfully in the domain of the labor movement. These problems are not amenable to solution by the remedies that WIA and TANF offer—nor, evidently, were they ever meant to be. The labor movement now discerns that the Bush administration's ultimate goal is not merely stopping what forward movement labor generated during AFL-CIO president John Sweeney's first years, but dismantling all the social structures put in place by the New Deal, including the FLSA of 1938 and Wagner-Peyser, the 1935 law that created the U.S. Employment Service.

WIA spending authority was to expire on September 30, 2003. In May 2003, according to the *Employment and Training Reporter* (2003b, 515), reauthorization was moving in the House and expected in the Senate. As of early 2004, the Senate bill was in conference committee. The debate revolves around an agenda that pushes costs as far down to the user as possible and reserves benefits for the employers. Should One-Stop infrastructure now be funded through partner contributions, not with state money? Should rules that prioritize services for people with multiple barriers to employment (the term for clients who are typically low-income with few marketable skills, female, and/or minority) be eased or waived? Could WIA programs be "doing more to meet employers' needs for trained workers" (*Employment and Training Reporter* 2002, 115). In the meantime, a GAO report summarized in the *Employment and Training Reporter* pointed out that although WIA prioritizes services to low-income clients, its funding is based 60 percent on the number of unemployed in a state and only 10 percent on the relative number of disadvantaged adults (2003c, 535).

Training is not the solution to poverty and the lack of good jobs. In a depressed economy, this mistake has consequences. Halfway through 2003, Adam Geller in the *Chicago Tribune* reported that the average time an unemployed worker now remained jobless was twenty weeks, nearly 22 percent of unemployed workers had been out for more than six months, and 13 percent had been out for a year or more. These times are the longest since 1983 (Geller 2003, 8). The jobs are simply not there; although the recession is commonly regarded as being over, employers are not hiring.

If the politics of the Workforce Investment Act were different, it could provide a great service in this new economy. Let us keep the One-Stops. The infrastructure of local job placement offices has been created. Partnerships have been negotiated. Computers have been purchased, carpets laid, caseworkers trained, the lights are on, and the phones are ringing. But let us change the eligibility requirements to serve on WIBs so that anyone can run, and let us allow people to elect representatives from each service area. Extend and increase unemployment compensation. Teach workers' rights and the right to collective bargaining in all training programs. But also reinvest in K–12 education so that "training" for adults does not mean basic literacy. The list could go on—we all have ideas about what should happen. This is a different set of social relationships, true; but the best kind of GI Bill for workers would be changing the politics so that we stopped the war.

References

Associated Press. 1998. "Clinton Signs Job-Training Bill." *Dubuque Telegraph Herald*, 8 August, A2.
Broder, David S. 1998. "Wellstone-DeWine Job Training Bill Deserves More Attention." *Wisconsin State Journal*, 5 August, 11A.

Employment and Training Reporter. 2002. "Federal Officials Lay Out Blueprints for Renewed WIA." 115.

———. 2003a. "Number of Trainees Dropped in Transition from JTPA to WIA." 501.

———. 2003b. "Stakeholders Oppose Wagner-Peyser Repeal on House Bill." 515.

———. 2003c. "WIA Funds Do Not Follow Workforce Needs, Says GAO." 535.

Fay, Robert, and Douglas Lippoldt. 1999. *The Public Employment Service in the United States.* Paris: Organization for Economic Co-Operation and Development Publications.

Federal Funds Information for States (FFIS). 2001. Table 1. Major Discretionary and Mandatory Program Funding. Available at www.ffis.org.

Gault, Barbara. 2002. "Utilizing Workforce Investment Act Programs and TANF to Provide Education and Training Opportunities to Reduce Poverty Among Low-Income Women." Testimony before the House Education and the Workforce Committee, Subcommittee on Twenty-First Century Competitiveness. March 12. Washington, DC: Institute for Women's Policy Research.

Geller, Adam. 2003. "Support Groups Flourish as Job-Seekers Founder." *Chicago Tribune*, 2 June, Sec. 4, 8.

General Accounting Office. 1994. "Multiple Employment Training Programs: Major Overhaul Is Needed." Clarence Crawford: statement before the subcommittee on Employment, Housing and Aviation. March 3, GAO/T-HEHS-94–109.

"Good Job: Federal System Was Dinosaur: Job Training Reform Good News for Workers." 1998. *Cincinnati Enquirer*, 11 August, A8.

Gunderson, Morley, and Andrew Sharpe. 1998. *Forging Business-Labor Partnerships: The Emergence of Sector Councils in Canada.* Toronto: University of Toronto Press, Center for the Study of Living Standards.

Joyce, Shannon. 1998. "Congress OK's DeWine's Job Training Bill." *Dayton Daily News*, City Edition, 1 August, 2B.

National Governors Association (NGA). 1997. "Current Investments in Incumbent Worker Training Leave Needs Unmet." Washington, DC: National Governors Association. Available at www.nga.org/Pubs/Issue Briefs/1997.

Schwartz, Robert M. 1999. *The Labor Law Source Book: Texts of Twenty Federal Labor Laws.* Cambridge, MA: Work Rights Press.

U.S. Department of Labor. 1999. *Report on the American Workforce 1999.* Washington, DC: U.S. Government Printing Office.

———. 2000. "Workforce Investment Act Final Rules." *Federal Register*, 11 August, 49294–464.

Weir, Margaret. 1992. *Politics and Jobs: The Boundaries of Employment Policy in the United States.* Princeton, NJ: Princeton University Press.

White House. 1998. "Remarks by the President at the Signing Ceremony for the Workforce Investment Act of 1998." Office of the Press Secretary, August 7.

Workforce Investment Act of 1998: Public Law 105–220. 112 Stat. 936. 105th Cong., 8 August 1998. Available at www.doleta.gov/youth_services/pdf.wialaw.txt.

Working for America Institute. 1999. *The Union Handbook for Workforce Investment Act Implementation.* Washington, DC: AFL-CIO Working for America Institute.

7

Revolving Doors

Temp Agencies as Accelerators of Churning in Low-Wage Labor Markets

Chirag Mehta and Nik Theodore

Throughout the 1990s, the temporary staffing industry (TSI) enjoyed phenomenal growth, becoming a major employer of low-wage workers, including former welfare recipients. Between 1993 and 2000, average daily employment in the industry increased by 92 percent from 1.32 million to 2.54 million jobs (Brogan 2001), a growth trajectory that was driven by increases in blue-collar employment, as well as by modest increases in clerical and professional placements (Belman and Golden 2000; Estevão and Lach 2000). By the close of the decade, the TSI had become an important gatekeeper in low-wage labor markets as the industry's business clients turned an increasing number of job vacancies over to temp agencies to be filled.

Optimistic accounts suggest that the low-commitment employment arrangements for which the TSI is well known may enhance opportunities for low-wage workers to readily enter the workforce because the ability to quickly replace underperforming workers lowers the potential risks faced by businesses employing these workers. In other words, employers might be more willing to accept welfare leavers and other low-wage workers at their worksites because temp agencies bear the costs associated with re-placing workers who do not perform adequately. If this is the case, tempo-rary staffing agencies might have a positive role to play in assisting workers in overcoming barriers to employment and career development.

However, there may be significant downsides to the flexible employment model promoted by temporary staffing agencies. In addition to the below-average wages associated with temping, employment in the industry appears to be inescapably cyclical. The TSI has established itself as a buffer during swings in the economy, expanding rapidly prior to macroeconomic upswings and contracting sharply as the economy slips into recession (Theodore and Peck 2002). This downside of flexibility was evident during the economic slowdown/recession that began in late 2000; in the first two quarters of the downturn, the TSI shed more than 661,000 jobs (BLS 2002). In the early months of the official recession, job losses in the TSI accounted for approximately half of all job losses nationwide. Hence, this relatively small sector shouldered the brunt of job losses as unemployment that occurred in manufacturing, construction, trade, and services industries was displaced onto the TSI and its workers.

In addition to performing as a cyclical buffer as the fortunes of the economy change, the TSI allows employers to rapidly adjust overall employment levels during periods of sustained growth. As a result, even during an economic recovery, employment in the TSI is subject to considerable volatility. In turn, this volatility places great demands on state unemployment insurance (UI) systems that are designed to deter employers from chronically laying off workers, thereby providing a measure of stability in local labor markets. The growing use of temporary staffing agencies by U.S. businesses may contribute to turbulence within low-wage labor markets as workers "churn" through temporary job slots and short-term assignments. There is a danger that as businesses increase their outsourcing of low-paying positions to the TSI, low-wage workers will cycle in and out of temp jobs, exacerbating the job insecurity and employment instability that characterizes low-wage employment generally and further undermining advancement opportunities and long-run wage progression for these workers. Extended periods in temp work, therefore, might trap workers in low-wage, secondary segments of the labor market that are disconnected from career ladders, cut off from higher-wage employment opportunities, and detached from unionized sectors of the economy.

This chapter explores the implications of worksite employers' increasing use of agency-supplied temps for the effectiveness of UI systems in deterring temporary layoffs. The next section reviews the efficacy of experience-rated UI tax systems in discouraging temporary layoffs. This is followed by an examination of the role of the TSI in employers' flexibility strategies and an analysis of the extent to which the TSI has relieved worksite employers of responsibilities for compensating unemployed workers. Using data from eight states with large numbers of temporary workers, we examine the extent to which the TSI absorbed rising UI claims during the 1993–2000 recovery.

Temp Agencies and Unemployment

The speed and intensity with which the TSI experienced job losses in the 2001 recession demonstrates that firms' use of agency-supplied temps has retained a pronounced cyclical sensitivity and that many firms use their temporary workforces as a rather blunt instrument for balancing labor demand and supply. Firms have turned to temporary staffing agencies to assist them in implementing strategies of labor flexibility, calling on agencies to perform functions that otherwise make it difficult for employers to independently carry out flexible staffing strategies on a large scale. Key among these is the efficient recruitment and immediate deployment of workers on an as-needed basis. Although some firms maintain lists of on-call workers and direct-hire temporaries who can be recalled on short notice, the costs associated with recruiting direct-hire temps can be substantial and additional costs may be incurred if job tasks are left unfinished while companies await needed workers. Staffing agencies help hold down these costs by performing the recruitment function and providing a ready source of workers for their clients.

A second crucial function concerns the legal responsibilities and costs associated with employing workers. Since most temporary staffing agencies are the legal employers of the workers they supply to business clients, they relieve clients of responsibilities and costs associated with payroll taxes and ensuring compliance with many of the legal safeguards that are in place to protect employees. Of particular importance is the role the TSI plays in relieving its business clients of the responsibility for contributing UI taxes for temporary workers. Like workers in standard employment arrangements, agency-supplied temps are eligible to collect UI if they meet employment and earnings thresholds. Temporary staffing agencies contribute UI taxes for the workers they supply to their business clients and, consequently, states hold agencies responsible when those workers claim UI benefits. Worksite employers, therefore, are free to adjust the size of their workforces without necessarily incurring rising UI costs.

Deterring Temporary Layoffs: Experience Rating UI Taxes

Generally, states will penalize employers that lay off workers who go on to claim UI benefits by increasing their UI tax rates. The system of calibrating employers' tax rates to their layoff experience is known as "experience rating." In part, the intent of experience rating UI tax rates is to deter employers from temporarily laying off their workforces. The effectiveness of the deterrence, however, may be compromised when staffing agencies become the legal employer of their clients' temporary workforces. When a worksite employer cancels an order for temporary workers and these workers become unemployed and claim UI benefits, the costs associated with UI compensation are borne directly by the staffing agency, not by the worksite employer. Thus, the UI tax in such cases does not operate as a disincentive to worksite employers intending to lay off their agency-supplied temps.

The experience-rating component of UI systems operates to reduce the incidence of layoffs in two related ways. First, experience-rating formulas impose costs for layoffs on employers, thereby creating a financial incentive for firms to reduce the size and frequency of layoffs. Second, these mechanisms ensure that tax contributions made by low-turnover firms do not subsidize high-turnover firms by setting each employer's tax rate at such a level that the employer's contributions cover the claims charged against its account. It is through these experience-rating provisions that state UI systems require firms to absorb some of the social costs of involuntary unemployment.

Experience-rated UI tax systems are designed to discourage layoffs by calibrating an employer's UI tax contributions to the rise and fall in the amount of UI benefit claims made by its laid-off employees relative to the size of the employer's remaining payroll. Generally, as the number of UI benefit claims increases, all else being equal, so too do the UI tax contributions paid by the former employers of UI claimants.

Research on the efficacy of UI tax systems indicates that experience rating reduces the incidence of temporary layoffs; experience rating acts as a penalty to firms that generate unemployment, inducing employers to adopt higher-wage, lower-turnover strategies (Albrecht and Vroman 1999; see also Card and Levine 1994; Moomaw 1998). Presumably, employers take into account the increased costs associated with layoffs. Employers would rather achieve efficiencies by paying workers higher wages to increase productivity than by laying off workers and absorbing higher UI costs.

Outsourcing the Costs of Unemployment

Under traditional employment arrangements, the experience-rating mechanisms of state UI systems operate to discourage chronic, temporary layoffs and to encourage "high road" business practices. In cases where layoffs are necessary, employers bear some of the associated costs and workers receive a reduced share of their previous earnings while searching for work. However, the introduction of temporary staffing agencies into the employment arrangement "decouples" the cause-and-effect relationship between the generation of unemployment and the costs of UI. The use of temporary staffing agencies allows worksite employers to externalize some of the costs of unemployment, particularly in cyclically volatile, high-turnover industries and in those occupations where high turnover is the norm. By outsourcing employment needs to the TSI, worksite employers are held harmless for spells of unemployment by agency-supplied temps. Instead, the benefits claimed by these workers are charged to the accounts of staffing agencies. The influence of experience-rating policy mechanisms that have been shown to generate positive labor market effects through their influence on employers' staffing strategies is thereby weakened.

The growing use of temporary-agency workers has consequently shifted a greater share of the costs for compensating unemployed workers "downstream" in the employment relationship—away from worksite employers and toward the TSI and its workforce. The magnitude of this shift during the period from 1993 to 2000 has been striking. Table 7.1 presents data on the percentage change in the number of UI weeks claimed from workers' "primary" employer, aggregated from eight states: Arizona, California, Florida, Illinois, Massachusetts, New York, Texas, and Washington.[1] These states were selected because they have a large TSI, collectively comprising 50 percent of temporary-agency (employment services) employment nationwide, permitting an analysis of the changing impact of UI on the temporary staffing industry and on the industries of some of its business clients. The data presented in Table 7.1 show that temporary staffing agencies became the primary employer of a growing proportion of UI claimants during the period from 1993 to 2000.[2] According to these estimates, UI weeks claimed by workers employed primarily by employment service agencies[3] *increased* by nearly 60 percent while, in every major industry group, UI weeks claimed *decreased* by between 16 and 47 percent.[4]

Table 7.1

Percent Change in UI Weeks Claimed by Industry Group, Selected States, 1993–2000

Industry	Percent change
Employment services	+60
Construction	−35
Manufacturing	−42
Wholesale trade	−29
Retail trade	−47
Transportation and warehousing	−16
Professional, scientific, and technical services	−32
Health care and social assistance	−12
Accommodation and food services	−44
Other services (except public administration)	−19
Administrative support (excluding employment services)	−25

Source: U.S. DOL ETA, 2001a.

Note: Estimates are based on benefit accuracy measurement (BAM) sample collected by the U.S. Department of Labor from state UI agencies. The states are: Arizona, California, Florida, Illinois, Massachusetts, New York, Texas, and Washington.

As these figures reveal, the distribution of the costs of compensating the unemployed is shifting strongly the direction of the TSI. Figure 7.1 illustrates the change in the distribution of total UI weeks claimed from 1993 to 2000 aggregated for the eight target states. The TSI (employment services) increased its share of total UI weeks claimed relative to the industries that are among the major users of agency-supplied temps.

By 2000, the employment service industry's share of total UI weeks claimed exceeded the share of weeks claimed charged to employers in the administrative support, transportation and warehousing, and accommodation and food service industries. Employment services also posted the largest increase (3 percent) in the share of total UI weeks claimed. Only administrative support establishments (excluding employment services), health care and social assistance, and transportation and warehousing witnessed an increased share in UI weeks claimed over the period. The remaining industry groups reduced their share of total UI weeks claimed. The manufacturing sector posted the largest absolute decline (−4 percent) in its share of total UI weeks claimed, while retail trade posted the largest percentage reduction (−26 percent) in its share.

Figure 7.1 **Share of Total Annual Weekly Claims by Industry of Primary Employers, Selected States, 1993 and 2000**

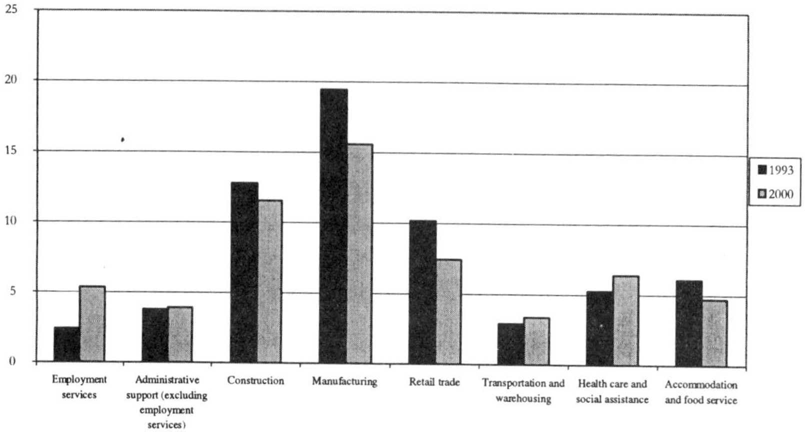

Note: The states are Arizona, California, Florida, Illinois, Massachusetts, New York, Texas, and Washington.

The magnitude of the shift in responsibility for compensating unemployed workers from worksite employers to the TSI is predictable considering that many (perhaps most) worksite employers employing temps "churn" these workers through job slots characterized by a high degree of turnover and frequent involuntary layoffs. Statistics on the job tenure of agency-supplied temps support results from employer surveys indicating that individual workers typically are employed at a given worksite on only a short-term basis. Approximately 45 percent of temporary workers spend, on average, less than six months on any single job assignment, while 72 percent worked for less than one year on a single assignment (Cohany 1996). In comparison, almost half of all workers hired permanently and directly by employers spend four years or more on the job. Workers in flexible arrangements (including agency-supplied temps) constitute approximately one-quarter of all workers, yet account for approximately 40 percent of workers with job tenures of less than one year (Cohany 1996). The intermittent nature of most temporary job assignments means that agency-supplied temps spend extended periods involuntarily unemployed and potentially eligible to collect UI benefits. Wayne Vroman's (1998) examination of UI recipiency rates for workers in nonstandard employment arrangements found that agency-supplied temps were unemployed at a rate of 40 percent compared to 10 percent for all adult workers.

Temp Agencies Shield Worksite Employers from Rising UI Costs

The displacement of UI costs onto the TSI by worksite employers might be minimized if temporary staffing agencies were able to pass these costs back on to business clients in the form of higher billing rates. However, in most markets, severe price competition between temporary staffing agencies significantly limits their ability do this—further insulating worksite employers from UI-related costs resulting from their flexible staffing arrangements. In some specialized niches of temporary help, such as markets for executives, scientists, and nurses where demand for workers consistently outpaces the supply of labor, temporary agencies may successfully charge higher billing rates and thus can more completely recover rising UI costs. But for the majority of temporary staffing agencies that primarily supply clerical and blue-collar workers, heightened competition in local labor markets (see Theodore and Peck 2002) has forced agencies to absorb higher UI costs.

Given the pricing strategies of the market leaders, this heightened price competition and downward pressures on margins are likely to continue. As John Bowmer, then the CEO of Adecco, the largest staffing company in the world, explained, "Certainly, one of the global trends that is out there and not likely to disappear soon is the trend to lower margins. In some part, this is the inevitable price to be paid for having higher visibility and bigger volumes with clients" (quoted in Staffing Industry Analysts 1999a). According to some industry analysts, large staffing agencies are culpable for intensifying price competition in the industry, a strategy analysts regard as an attempt to force out of business marginal competitors that are less able to absorb rising costs. Adecco is only one of several large, publicly held staffing agencies that has been accused by its competitors of creating strong downward pressures on billing rates. Manpower Inc. too has been widely criticized for cutting billing rates to "[go] for share over profit" in certain markets (Staffing Industry Analysts 1999b). Falling gross margins for some of the largest corporate players in the staffing industry, such as Adecco, Kelly Services, and Manpower, appear to support allegations that this strategy is being followed. In 2000, Adecco reported gross margins of 18.7 percent, while Kelly Services and Manpower reported margins of 17.6 percent and 18 percent, respectively (Staffing Industry Analysts 2001). Since 1992, gross margins for Kelly Services and Manpower have declined from nearly 22 percent to their current levels.

Price competition in the light industrial and clerical segments of the staffing industry—segments that account for 67 percent of the TSI's placements—has driven billing rates and gross margins to surprisingly low levels (Brogan 2001). Table 7.2 presents estimates of billing rates and average gross margins (bill rate per hour for temporary workers less total labor costs) for four occupations: data entry clerks, shipping and receiving clerks, helper/production workers, and secretaries. These figures do not account for operating expenses outside of the direct costs of compensating temporary workers, so actual margins will be even narrower than the 12 to 22 percent estimated in Table 7.2.

Because of intense price competition, temporary staffing agencies have few avenues through which to recover increased UI expenses from their clients. Agencies' cost recovery strategies therefore must rely on reducing the costs of doing business by containing administrative costs, holding down wages paid to temporary workers, and limiting future UI claims in order to minimize UI tax rates. The imperative to control costs may explain efforts on the part of industry representatives to pass regulations at the state level to make it more difficult for agency-supplied temps to collect UI benefits. The American Staffing Association (ASA), the main industry association, has advocated a model unemployment insurance policy with considerable success (NATSS 1999). This model policy requires temporary workers to return to their temporary staffing agency upon completion of job assignments and accept "suitable" employment or else be ineligible for UI benefits. Of the eight states examined here, Florida, Illinois, and Texas have adopted a version of ASA's UI policy either through regulation, administrative order, or by statute. Approximately twenty-three other states have adopted the policy as well (NELP 2001).

UI Costs Are Displaced onto the Temporary Workforce

Worksite employers displace UI costs associated with their contingent workforce onto the TSI. In turn, the TSI displaces some of these costs onto the temporary workforce. Wayne Vroman (1998) found that agency-supplied temps experience the lowest UI recipiency rates compared to other contingent workers (independent contractors, part-time workers, and on-call workers) and all adult workers regardless of type of employment contract. In 1994, the average UI recipiency rate (defined as the number of workers receiving unemployment compensation relative to

Table 7.2

Estimated Gross Margins on Temporary Workers

Data entry clerk
Bill rate ($ per hour)		$13.21
Median wage ($ per hour)	$9.09	
Legally required benefits	$1.32	
Total labor costs		($10.41)
Gross margin (bill rate—total labor costs)		$2.80
		21% of bill rate

Shipping and receiving clerk
Bill rate		$12.20
Median wage	$8.99	
Legally required benefits	$1.30	
Total labor costs		($10.29)
Gross margin (bill rate—total labor costs)		$1.91
		16% of bill rate

Helper/production worker
Bill rate		$9.35
Median wage	$7.19	
Legally required benefits	$1.04	
Total labor costs		($8.23)
Gross margin (bill rate—total labor costs)		$1.12
		12% of bill rate

Secretary
Bill rate		$15.63
Median wage	$10.69	
Legally required benefits	$1.55	
Total labor costs		($12.24)
Gross margin (bill rate—total labor costs)		$3.39
		22% of bill rate

Sources: Wage rates were obtained from the Bureau of Labor Statistics Occupational Employment Survey (2000); billing rates were obtained from Institute of Management and Administration, Inc. (1999); and estimates of legally required benefits are based on Wiatrowski, 1999.

the total number of unemployed workers) for all workers twenty-five years and older was 39 percent. For agency-supplied temps, this figure was only 28 percent. Furthermore, agency-supplied temps receive UI compensation at lower rates relative to rates for workers in industries representing the largest users of temporary staffing services. Vroman found that UI recipiency was 46 percent for all manufacturing workers (sixteen years and older) and 34 percent for all clerical and sales work-

Table 7.3

Occupational Distribution in the Personnel Supply Service Industry, 1999

Occupation	Total staffing industry employment	Share of total staffing industry employment (percent)	Median wage (dollars)
Laborers and freight, stock, and material movers	292,100	7.7	7.32
Office clerks, general	271,730	7.2	8.99
Packers and packagers, hand	182,070	4.8	6.87
Helpers/production workers	170,380	4.5	7.19
Data entry keyers	140,740	3.7	9.09
Health care practitioners and technical occupations	129,010	3.4	20.15
Secretaries, except legal, medical, and executive	120,790	3.2	10.69
Sales and related occupations	118,780	3.1	10.86
Customer service representatives	109,660	2.9	9.82
Receptionists and information clerks	91,990	2.4	9.00
Total	1,627,250	42.9	

Source: Bureau of Labor Statistics, Occupational Employment Survey (2000).

ers, both substantially greater than the 28 percent recipiency rate for temp workers.

Several reasons explain why agency-supplied temps experience lower UI recipiency rates relative to workers in standard employment relationships. First, many (48 percent) agency-supplied temps work full-time but for only part of the year, making it difficult for them to meet earnings thresholds that in part determine benefit eligibility (authors' calculations from the March supplement to the Current Population Survey [CPS] 1993–2000). Of these workers, only 15 percent received UI benefits during their current spell of unemployment. Second, agency-supplied temps often are low-wage workers, compounding the difficulty they face in meeting earnings thresholds (Table 7.3). According to a study by the General Accounting Office (2000) examining the role UI plays as a safety net for workers, low-wage workers were twice as likely to be out of work as higher-wage workers, but only half as likely to receive UI benefits.

Conclusion

The continuing growth of the TSI has been fueled by demands by worksite employers for workers employed under flexible employment arrangements. This has drawn increasing numbers of workers into temporary employment arrangements where they are assigned by temp agencies to jobs on an as-needed basis. This chapter has examined one outcome of the growing use of agency-supplied temps—the displacement of the costs for unemployment insurance from worksite employers onto the TSI and its workforce. It has been shown that many industries have effectively outsourced their unemployment and its associated costs to the TSI and, in the process, have undermined the intent of experience-rated UI systems. For workers, this has meant that local labor markets are further destabilized as the effectiveness of experience-rating provisions in state UI systems in deterring layoffs has been undermined. The result is increased turbulence in labor markets, even during a robust economic expansion. Unless policy makers reform state UI systems to account for the increased prevalence of UI claims made by the former employees of the TSI, worksite employers will continue to externalize the costs of unemployment, thereby reducing employment tenures and increasing turnover in local labor markets.

To remedy this failure of UI policy to respond adequately to rising UI claims made by workers placed by the TSI, states should consider revising UI policy instruments to internalize the UI-related costs of laying off agency-supplied temps within the operating budgets of worksite employers. For example, states could require worksite employers to contribute UI taxes for procured agency-supplied temps. Under such a policy, states would charge UI claims made by temporary workers to the accounts of worksite employers where they held their primary job assignment. Temporary staffing agencies could continue to perform payroll functions for their clients and shoulder legal and financial responsibility for other areas of employment law. However, worksite employers would carry the responsibility for insuring procured agency-supplied temps against involuntary unemployment.

A second option would be to weight UI tax rates of worksite employers that use temporary staffing agencies to account for the UI-claims experience of the TSI. Some states weight employers' UI tax rates to account for the UI-claims experience of the industry in which they operate, the reason being that the risk of unemployment within an entire industry is reflected to some degree upon all the firms that constitute that industry. Similarly, worksite employers are responsible for a significant share of the risk of unemployment within the TSI.

Minimally, states should address the extremely low UI recipiency rates of temporary-agency workers by altering eligibility requirements. Expanding UI eligibility among agency-supplied temps will help job seekers search for permanent and more stable employment while more significantly internalizing the costs of UI within employers' operating budgets. States also should target inherent biases against unemployed temporary agency workers in UI rules (see NELP 2001 for a discussion of policy alternatives for restoring the UI safety net for contingent workers) by increasing benefit levels, reducing earnings thresholds to expand eligibility, and changing voluntary quit rules to allow search for full-time work rather than returning to the staffing agency for assignment.

The types of policy reforms described above are necessary in order to establish a floor under temporary labor markets. Throughout the 1990s, the temporary staffing industry became an important employer of former welfare recipients and other low-wage workers. Welfare leavers were channeled in large numbers into the contingent workforce by local welfare programs operating a "work first" approach to welfare reform that was guided by the belief that "any job is a good job" (see Peck and Theodore 2001). For these workers, however, job opportunities in the temp industry are accompanied by significant downsides; although employers have been willing to expand job offerings for temporary workers, these jobs have been associated with low wages and pronounced employment insecurity. Policy reforms that shift some of the costs of unemployment back "upstream" in the employment relationship are needed to ensure that temporary staffing agencies provide workers with quality employment opportunities without undermining stability in already turbulent low-wage labor markets.

Notes

Funding for this research was provided by the Ford Foundation. Thanks to Louise Simmons and Manny Ness for comments on an earlier draft of this chapter.

1. Some states charge UI claims to workers' last employers rather than their primary employer during the base period. The shift in UI claims charged to workers'

last employers closely resembles the shift in UI claims across primary employers as seen in Table 7.1.

2. Unemployment insurance is distributed to eligible unemployed workers on a weekly basis. At the time of the initial claim, a determination is made as to which of the workers' previous employers is responsible for the unemployment. The Benefit Accuracy Measurement (BAM) population includes payments from the State UI, Unemployment Compensation for Federal Employees (UCFE) (federal civilian), and Unemployment Compensation for Ex-Service Personnel (UCX) (military) unemployment compensation programs. The estimates do not indicate the number of persons that claimed the total number of UI weeks. According to statisticians at the U.S. Department of Labor (DOL) Employment Training Administration, the average duration of UI weeks was approximately 12 weeks claimed for agency-supplied temps and 13.6 weeks for all other workers (U.S. DOL ETA, 2001b). The estimates also do not indicate whether the last or primary employer was charged for the UI claim.

3. "Employment services" defined by the North American Industry Classification System includes employment placement agencies, temporary help services, and employee leasing services. In 1999, temporary help services accounted for approximately 70 percent of all employment in the employment services industry nationwide.

4. The average annual percentage change in weeks claimed was negative for all major industry groups. Employment services posted a 4 percent annual change in weeks claimed.

References

Albrecht, James, and Susan Vroman. 1999. "Unemployment Compensation Finance and Efficiency Wages." *Journal of Labor Economics* 17, no. 1: 141–67.
Belman, Dale, and Lonnie Golden. 2000. "Nonstandard and Contingent Employment: Contrasts by Job Type, Industry and Occupation." In *Nonstandard Work: The Nature and Challenges of Changing Employment Arrangements*, ed. Françoise Carré, Marianne Ferber, Lonnie Golden, and Stephen Herzenberg, 167–212. Champaign, IL: Industrial Relations Research Association.
BLS (Bureau of Labor Statistics). 2000. Occupational Employment Survey, Industry Staffing Patterns. U.S. data available at www.bls.gov/oes/oes_dl.htm (April 28, 2001).
———. 2002. "Employment Situation: January 2002" (www.bls.gov/news.release/empsit.nr0.htm).
Brogan, Timothy W. 2001. "Scaling New Heights: ASA's Annual Analysis of the Staffing Industry." Washington, DC: American Staffing Association.
Card, David, and Philip Levine. 1994. "Unemployment Insurance Taxes and the Cyclical and Seasonal Properties of Unemployment." *Journal of Public Economics* 53, no. 1: 1–29.
Cohany, Sharon. 1996. "Workers in Alternative Employment Arrangements." *Monthly Labor Review* 121, no. 11 (October): 31–45.
Estevão, Marcello, and Saul Lach. 2000. "The Evolution of Demand for Temporary Help Supply Employment in the United States." In *Nonstandard Work: The Nature*

and Challenges of Changing Employment Arrangements, ed. Françoise Carré, Marianne Ferber, Lonnie Golden, and Stephen Herzenberg, 123–44. Champaign, IL: Industrial Relations Research Association.

GAO (General Accounting Office). 2000. *Unemployment Insurance: Role as Safety Net for Low-Wage Workers Is Limited*. Washington, DC: U.S. General Accounting Office, December.

Institute of Management and Administration (IOMA), Inc. 1999. *Setting and Managing'Hourly Compensation Reference Guide*. IOMA's Report on Hourly Compensation. New York: Institute of Management and Administration.

Lenz, Edward. 1997. *Employer Liability Issues in Third-Party Staffing Arrangements*. Alexandria, VA: National Association of Temporary Staffing Services Publication.

Moomaw, Ronald. 1998. "Experience Rating and the Generosity of Unemployment Insurance: Effects on County and Metropolitan Unemployment Rates." *Journal of Labor Research* 19, no. 3: 543–60.

NATSS (National Association of Temporary Staffing Services). 1999. *NATSS Model Temporary Help Unemployment Insurance Law*, obtained from NATSS research staff.

NELP (National Employment Law Project). 2001. *Temp Work and Unemployment Insurance—Helping Employees at Temporary Staffing and Employee Leasing Agencies*. New York: National Employment Law Project, Inc.

Peck, Jamie, and Nik Theodore. 2000. "Work First: Welfare-to-Work and the Regulation of Contingent Labour Markets." *Cambridge Journal of Economics* 24, no. 1: 119–38.

Staffing Industry Analysts. 1999a. "Editor's Report—Adecco SA CEO John Bowmer's Keynote Speech to the Eighth Annual Staffing Industry Executive Forum." *SI Report* 6, 30 March: 9.

———. 1999b. "Editor's Report—Mitchell Fromstein's Retirement and the Promotion of Jeffrey Joerres to CEO May Portend a Strategic Shift at Manpower Inc." *SI Report* 9, 11 May: 8.

———. 2001. "Public Staffing Company Sales Growth Slows to 14% in 2000." *SI Report* 8, 27 April: 10–11.

Theodore, Nik, and Jamie Peck. 2002. "The Temporary Staffing Industry: Growth Imperatives and Limits to Contingency." *Economic Geography* 78, no. 4: 463–93.

U.S. Department of Labor, Employment and Training Administration (U.S. DOL ETA). 2001a. Unpublished data.

———. 2001b. Unpublished data.

Vroman, Wayne. 1998. *Labor Market Changes and Unemployment Insurance Benefit Availability*. Washington, DC: U.S. Department of Labor.

Wiatrowski, William. 1999. "Tracking Changes in Benefit Costs." *Compensation and Working Conditions* 4, no. 1 (Spring): 32–37.

III

Labor and the Struggles over Social Welfare and Work

8

Evaluating the Living-Wage Strategy

Prospects, Problems, and Possibilities

David J. Olson and Erich Steinman

Living-wage campaigns have captured the imagination of organizations that represent low-wage workers. These campaigns succeeded in establishing more than eighty governmental ordinances by 2002, a number that grew to over a hundred by June 2003. The campaigns illuminate the possibility and importance of coalitions among labor movement, community, and religious organizations. This is significant given the immense animosity that has characterized these relationships in the past decades. Coalition building is always difficult and coalitions fragile, even when the partners are similar, as in the case of labor unions and civil rights groups, and especially if they are dissimilar, as in the case of the variety of groups involved in the World Trade Organization protests (Levi and Olson 2000; McAdam 1982; Levi and Murphy 2003).

That there are so many thriving campaigns and that most involve real coalitions among labor, community, and religious partners confirm the existence of a social movement involving numerous individuals and groups throughout the country in sustained collective actions aimed at winning living-wage legislation and monitoring its enforcement after enactment. The existence of so many ordinances indicates the success of this movement in achieving its immediate goals and raises important issues about the future prospects, problems, and possibilities of this strategy for raising the standard of living for working people in the United States.

In this chapter we analyze important achievements of living-wage campaigns and their potential impacts by assessing the strengths and limits such campaigns display. We focus initially on the content of living-wage ordinances to assess what has been achieved. We then examine the actors involved in campaign coalitions, the barriers they confront and, despite formidable obstacles, the living-wage prospects that animate the movement. We interpret the outcomes of these campaigns by examining the nature and timing of ordinance adoption, as well as recurring patterns and processes involved in their enactment. We conclude by providing an evaluation of the prospects, limits, and potential strengths of the living-wage campaign.

Content of Living-Wage Ordinances: What Has Been Achieved?

Since the mid-1990s, cities and counties have passed living-wage ordinances that require private sector firms that have financial relationships to government, either as service contractors, recipients of subsidies or tax breaks, concessionaires, tenants on publicly owned property, or direct government employees to provide a "living wage," a wage above the federally mandated minimum wage. Elsewhere, Levi, Olson, and Steinman (2002–2003) provide an up-to-date cumulative description of living-wage ordinances passed around the country. That snapshot gives a sense of the nature, scale, scope, and distribution of these ordinances. While the number of living-wage laws continues to change, their overall characteristics remain similar. For this reason, we draw heavily upon that source and here present information up to 2002.

As of June 2002 there were over eighty ordinances on the books, counting precursors in Des Moines, Iowa (1988, amended 1996) and Gary, Indiana (1991). Sixty-five ordinances had passed since Baltimore's in 1994, generally considered the first victory in the modern living-wage movement.

Definitions of what constitutes a "living wage" vary widely across adopting communities. Before their repeal, for example, wages ranged from $6.15 (New Orleans) to $11.42 an hour assuming the employer pays health benefits, otherwise $12.92 an hour (Santa Monica). Many are indexed to inflation or to the federally determined poverty level. Job categories covered typically include janitorial, food service, security, parking lot, hotel, restaurant, and clerical workers. However, a few ordinances cover more categories; for example, Chicago includes home health care workers and Denver on-site child care workers.

Thirty-five ordinances principally cover city or county service contractors. Nine cover only some form of economic development subsidy. Twenty-four cover both service contracts and economic
development subsidies. Seven ordinances additionally cover some firms
leasing land from the city, and one ordinance, in Berkeley, extends
coverage to all businesses within the Berkeley Marina Zone. Several
also cover direct city or county employees in addition to contracts
and/or subsidies recipients.

One ordinance, in Santa Monica, required employers who had no
direct financial relationship with the city to pay a living wage (employers operating within the city's Coastal Zone tourist district with revenues of more than $5 million a year). Another ordinance, adopted in
New Orleans by referendum, extended more broadly in covering all public
and private sector workers, thus resembling the more familiar minimum
wage. Twenty ordinances cover some nonprofits.

Eleven ordinances include some "jobs" language—e.g., job creation
goals or targeted community hiring. Two require covered firms to work
with community hiring halls to fill jobs created with city contracts or
development subsidies.

Fifty-two ordinances require (or encourage) some form of health benefits. This sometimes implies only that the health benefit requirement is
simply stated as such but can also require a wage at a higher percentage
of the poverty calculation for firms that do not provide health benefits.
Eight include vacation benefits. Many ordinances include specific labor
language having to do with prevailing wage, participation in union apprenticeship programs, prohibitions on use of public money for antiunion activities, worker retention, sick pay, vacation pay, and health care.

Context of Living-Wage Campaigns: Actors, Barriers, and Prospects

Actors and Joint Action

Living-wage legislation is generally initiated by either community-based
organizations—such as the IAF (Industrial Area Foundation), ACORN
(Association of Community Organizations for Reform Now), and a wide
range of local churches and neighborhood associations—or by labor
unions, either particular unions or central labor councils (CLCs). Successful campaigns seem to require the involvement of both types of or-

ganizations from the very beginning. It is hard to bring a missing partner aboard once the action has begun. Without the proper base in both the unions and the community, the campaign is less likely to be successful and the changes less likely to be sustained. These campaigns are also more likely to succeed if they are bottom up. This ensures continued demands for enforcement of legislation from those affected as well as contributing to the long-term construction of social networks and common interests that can be mobilized for future actions. If the campaign succeeds due to the joint efforts of community, faith-based, and labor organizations, they develop greater commitment to and monitoring of ongoing policy and confidence in their capacity to make future change (Lipsky and Levi 1972; Levi 2001; Fine 2001).

Labor Organizations

Labor's reasons for joining living-wage coalitions derive from several factors. The labor movement, reeling from membership declines, is eager to attract new members. As part of its recruitment strategy, the "new leadership" of the AFL-CIO, elected in 1996, developed a Union Cities program, to revitalize the role of unions in political and economic development. Labor's support for the living wage allows it to target previously ignored employment sectors, such as low-wage service sectors where women and people of color predominate, as well as employee groups whose employers have been particularly resistant to union organizing (Bronfenbrenner et al. 1998).

Labor's recent organizing among low-income communities brings union organizers into direct contact with traditional community organizers in these same communities. Due to labor's recent efforts to involve members of low-income communities, organizers increasingly draw upon younger people who practiced organizing in social movements at the neighborhood level (Voss and Sherman 2000). The alliances between labor and community have developed livable wage standards as an actionable agenda item (Zabin and Martin 1999). The new coalitions have also been critical for overcoming long-standing antagonisms between community and labor activists. The racism and sexism of many unions, their conflicting goals when it comes to urban renewal and other large construction projects that displace the poor without employing them, and their past indifference to service sector workers have proved an obstacle to organizing the very workers that the

AFL-CIO now recognizes as providing the potential for the highest membership growth.

Living-wage ordinances also help unions by setting norms about prevailing local wage levels. If employers are to compete for workers they are forced to offer employees higher pay. The living-wage ordinance also empowers unionized city and county workers. In an era of privatization, where unionized public workforces see their numbers dwindling due to outsourcing of their work, forcing contractors to pay living wages to their private employees levels the cost competition between public and private provision of services. Living-wage laws make it less tempting for cities to privatize service provision, thus increasing union bargaining power.

From the labor movement's point of view, the living-wage campaigns are most likely to be successful and sustained when linked with organizing drives, which mean that even failures in passing legislation can represent labor movement gains. Targeting living-wage proposals to cover employees in firms where employers have blocked workers' attempts to organize attracts labor to the campaigns. In Houston, the ordinance lost citywide but won in low-wage neighborhoods. Moreover, the joint campaign with Service Employees International Union (SEIU) Local 100 helped the union succeed in its efforts to organize Head Start workers. In New Orleans, the community-labor coalition targeted hotel workers, which then became the focus of an organizing drive by Hotel and Restaurant Employees (HERE). The New Orleans campaign began in reaction to efforts by hotels, restaurants, and other hospitality industries to block unionization activities led by SEIU. In Santa Monica the living wage would have covered employees of major beachfront employers who previously resisted unionization. In Oakland, where the ordinance passed in 1998, the effect was to frighten the Port Authority, which was not covered due to provisions of the city charter. Four years later, in 2002, the living-wage coalition remobilized to pass Measure I, extending living-wage coverage to port employees.

Religious Organizations

Religious organizations are active in most, but not all, living-wage campaigns. Besides providing occasions for demonstrating visible concern for the welfare needs of the poor and communities of color, living-wage campaigns satisfy organizational maintenance and enhancement needs of religious organizations. They provide opportunities for recruiting and retaining members within the inner-city neighborhoods by making the religious groups relevant to their needs. The campaigns also afford churches and synagogues opportunities to form alliances with community groups whose membership is partly shared, thus demonstrating solidarity on social and political issues. In addition, the campaigns offer direct community engagement in neighborhoods where churches and synagogues historically have been located, but where large shares of their membership no longer reside.

Congregations, parishes, and synagogues at the neighborhood level are represented city- and county-wide by councils of churches or diocese and synagogue associations that have been particularly active as coalition members. They act as advocacy groups promoting the living wage. They find allies who share their membership, they provide an outlet for direct action for their activist members, and they develop social networks that prove beneficial in their ongoing social service delivery activities.

Besides lending legitimacy and authority to living-wage campaigns, religious group involvement provides significant contributions to organization building for campaigns. Church and synagogue involvement allows preexisting religious group resources to be deployed in organizing efforts and expanded through social network linkages. Churches and synagogues provide meeting places for campaign organizers and participants, they recruit campaign activists from membership rolls, provide venues for leadership training, offer financial and technical resources, and assist in developing social networks spanning neighborhood to citywide levels.

Community Organizations

National community-based organizations, such as IAF and ACORN, have resources and commitments to devise new and workable strategies for building a social movement of poor people. In addition to the potential of living-wage laws to advance these groups' social goals, they greatly benefit from highly visible participation in successful public campaigns such as living-wage efforts. Their legitimacy and funding is derived exclusively from efforts to mobilize community members for desired changes. Unlike churches, they have no other rationale for existence, and unlike successful unions, they cannot make legal claims to represent workers in formal negotiations over wages and other work issues. Community organizations lack structured opportunities for the maintenance of member participation (such as job sites for unions). Nor do they receive support as a by-product of deeply institutionalized behavior such as attending church or paying union dues. Thus, community organizations must be highly responsive to community members' needs as they compete for participation and support. Perhaps even more so than other coalition members, national community organizations with local chapters must be entrepreneurs, capable of quickly adopting campaign strategies that have proven successful elsewhere. With generally fewer ties to formal hierarchies and dependent on street-level participation, community organizations have much to gain from living-wage campaigns, particularly those that generate substantial publicity about their positive contribution.

Several secular developments have also fueled community organization involvement in living-wage campaigns. Among these are the steep reduction in government funding for welfare programs and poverty programs. This has forced low-income groups to articulate their own agendas from the bottom up and has led to a search for allies from labor and religious organizations in pursuing new agendas. Community organizations' focus on the availability of jobs, the access their members have to the workforce, and the quality of employment (including living-wage standards) have brought them more directly in contact with unions. The early history of living-wage campaigns initiated by ACORN or IAF did not necessarily involve unions, however. This has largely changed. Some of the campaigns in which ACORN has been involved were initiated by central labor councils (e.g., in San Jose and Detroit), and some by union locals and ACORN together (e.g., in Cook County, Illinois), but all ultimately required a joint partnership and commitment of resources.

Barriers

A decade of successes for living-wage campaigns is remarkable given the numerous and powerful barriers to ordinance enactment. The distinctly local nature of the campaigns provides an initial barrier. Decentralized social movements locate the arena for action among neighborhoods, cities, counties, and special districts. Lacking a hierarchy of coordination, local campaigns start nearly anew with each successive locale. They lack a template for action and must construct their own strategies, tactics, and coalitional partners. The considerable variation in the particulars of ordinance coverage, compensation levels, whistle blower protections, and enforcement devices derives from localized circumstances. Nationally linked organizations (ACORN, IAF) do provide important information and advice, but the living-wage movement remains emphatically a local campaign.

Locally based living-wage campaigns create incentives for opponents to appeal to higher-level governments to preempt or to nullify living-wage ordinances, particularly in communities where such laws enjoy broad popular support, but where such support is not present within higher-level governments. This barrier appears in two forms. First, those opposed to living-wage laws can turn to state legislatures and governors who may be less supportive of legislating living wages than are local officials. This form of preemption occurred in Oregon and at least four other states. Within these states, not only are existing living-wage ordinances nullified, but current and future campaigns are defused by preemption. Second, opponents of living-wage laws can seek judicial relief by appealing successful enactments in state courts. This occurred in New Orleans, after a sweeping minimum wage law passed by 63 percent to 37 percent in 2002.

Social movements fighting for low-wage workers predictably find themselves lacking conventional resources that are crucial to influencing public policy. This is particularly so where targeted firms and employer groups are resource rich and have material interests at stake in the conflict. The time, money, personnel, access to media, and related resources required for building or deflecting agendas and influencing policy makers are most often unevenly distributed in local communities and represent a significant barrier to be overcome in campaigns for low-wage workers.

The framing of the living-wage issue for public consumption and official action confronts similar obstacles. Living-wage advocates appeal to norms of civic fairness. They argue the immorality of less than self-sustaining wages paid to publicly contracted workers and employees of government-assisted firms. This appeal to the civic conscience is contested by groups opposed to living-wage laws. Opponents are often joined by public officials allied with employer groups and assisted by negative media portrayals of the living-wage campaign. The ostensible strength of the conscience-based appeal for fairness can also be transformed into a weakness in campaigns. When advocates of the living wage rely upon appeals to fairness, they often forgo familiar social movement tactics of direct action, boycott, or withholding patronage.

Coalitions of labor, religious, and community organizations meld unlike groups in collective action where the ties uniting the groups are often fragile, tense, and of uncertain duration. Groups composing the coalition often lack a past history of working together in common cause (Nissen 1999). Both their past histories and divergent immediate interests pose barriers to be surmounted in coalition campaigns for ordinance enactment. The coalitions also experience difficulties in sustaining themselves following enactment when the immediate goal is attained. With achievement, coalition partners may return to their own and more direct organizational enhancement and maintenance needs. This occurs during the crucial implementation stage, when monitoring and enforcement of the ordinance requires coalition attention and action to sustain the intent of the law, or to defend bureaucratic action consistent with the law, or to renew sunset laws, or to extend the conditions and terms of the law. Only the most inclusive and cohesive coalitions persist in monitoring the implementation and enforcement of living-wage laws. Even where coalitions remain strong, the costs of noncompliance by firms covered by living-wage laws are often trivial and easy to absorb.

Most living-wage campaigns do not actively include beneficiaries of the ordinances as primary or even secondary participants. Social movements similarly composed have difficulties sustaining themselves. Absent a strong and attentive constituent base of ordinance beneficiaries, social movements generally experience a waning of interest, or membership attrition, or the replacement of one movement agenda with another (Pierson 1994).

The economic cycle experienced in local and regional economies poses a final obstacle. It is comparatively easier for local governments to meet the demands of living-wage advocates during periods of economic well-being, but it is more difficult when the economic cycle is depressed. A related irony is that communities with a prosperous economic base, e.g., Santa Cruz, may experience less difficulty in promoting living-wage laws than cities lacking a strong local economy where the needs of low-wage workers are more severe and persistent.

Prospects

Even with these barriers, however, a tremendous amount of effort has been directed to living-wage campaigns, as demonstrated by the striking number of successes. Why have this strategy and these campaigns generated such interest? Why have so many activists been attracted to the living-wage movement?

One factor is that the living-wage movement is a progressive success amid conservative political retrenchment characterized by increasing polarization of wealth and poverty, diminishing federal actions to alleviate poverty and inequality. Indeed, the most conspicuous statistic in the literature on the living-wage movement may be the growing number of ordinances passed nationwide. This reflects both the paucity of data regarding more material effects of these ordinances but also the striking nature of such a trend given the political climate. Understandably, progressive activists from a broad swath of issues and organizations are drawn to such a winning and publicized phenomenon. Also implicated in such local victories is the possibility of disrupting established local politics and opening up new angles of influence, as reported by a number of campaigns. However, the enthusiasm for the living-wage movement goes deeper than the attraction of a winning strategy and also appears to come from sources beyond discrete organizational self-interest. This interest is motivated by perceptions that the living-wage movement could significantly facilitate larger and longer-lasting changes that speak to moral and justice concerns shared by individuals within labor, community, and religious organizations as well as many outside these groups.

That the living-wage movement inspires hope for changes sought by the larger progressive movement (as it is) can be seen in claims made by living-wage campaigns, other advocates, and interested observers. Perhaps surprisingly, direct wage gains for workers and a reduction in poverty are not usually what partisans emphasize as the most exciting outcome of the living-wage phenomenon. While attention to these beneficial consequences is ubiquitous, and organizers make such issues central to campaigns, advocates and allies often acknowledge that the number of workers affected by these laws is relatively small (as suggested by virtually all pre- and postordinance studies). Similarly, advocates occasionally acknowledge that the overall impact on poverty is likely quite minimal (findings again supported by most studies). While insisting that these concrete, albeit limited, gains from living-wage policies are extremely important to the affected individuals, advocates also make clear that the import of the movement may be found in outcomes not yet realized. As Chapman (2002) notes in his enthusiastic review of the living-wage movement, which he dubs the "brightest star" of progressive politics, "The living wage movement continues to gather momentum as much because of its prospects as its accomplishments."

These prospects can be roughly captured by three main themes. The first prospect, as suggested by the heading of a descriptive article on the Living Wage Resource Center's Web site, is the possibility of "Building Power in our Workplaces and Neighborhoods." The novel element here is establishing—or reestablishing—a link between specific, geographically identifiable communities suffering from poverty, underemployment, and unemployment, on one hand, and workplaces, labor processes, and labor organizing on the other. This link was central to the organizing strategy and structure of the pioneering living-wage campaign in Baltimore (Fine 2001). Rather than community and labor being completely independent social locations and struggles, with antipoverty efforts detached from labor organizing, living-wage campaigns may allow claims and resources from these two spheres to be combined to generate an outcome greater, rather than lesser, than the sum of the component parts. Put differently, effectively linking antipoverty and labor issues represents a two-flank strategy for efforts to build concrete manifestations of power, a new, flexible, and proactive configuration that might extend beyond both the company gate and community boundaries. Advocates from labor, community, and religious organizations generally cast the process as a win-win dynamic for all parties, suggesting that each group may use living-wage campaigns to organize and boost membership. Thus the component parts as well as the overall multiorganizational and multiconstituency efforts may benefit.

A second prospect is the potential for renewing and invigorating public discussion of economic inequality and the implicit norms underlying regulation of economic activity. Living-wage campaigns introduce a bottom-up perspective for considering what factors are important in assessing economic issues in general and regulatory activity in particular. As Champlin and Knoedler (2002) argue in support of living wages, "imposing a living wage" threatens an understanding of economic prosperity "that has come to be defined almost exclusively in terms of a rising stock market and the accumulation of financial wealth." The living-wage movement is thus cast as a potential source for broadened and deepened public discourse regarding public economic interests beyond the formal scope of living-wage ordinances. A number of specific dimensions of living-wage policies are frequently linked to this type of project, such as increasing corporate accountability vis-à-vis public funds, challenging privatization and outsourcing, and prioritizing "high road" economic development strategies generating "good" jobs.

By far the greatest excitement, however, is linked to a third prospective accomplishment, the potential of the living-wage movement to create and sustain new and diverse coalitions. David Reynolds writes, "What makes the living-wage movement significant is the broad spectrum of local groups that it brings together" (Reynolds 1999, 66), a perspective frequently noted in the literature by and about the living-wage movement. While clearly rooted in the potential for "building power" as discussed above, this coalition-building development includes different elements and goes beyond community-labor links. One possibility is the extension of living-wage organizing campaigns into efforts that generate ongoing organizational structures, target new and expanding goals, and continue other formal collaborations. More generally, however, activists seem to imply that the potential goes beyond these specific efforts, sometimes referring to these coalitions in ways that hint at hopes of a more fundamental restructuring of the relationships among coalition members writ large. The Living Wage Resource Center Web site refers to the potential of the living-wage movement to generate coalitions that "promote greater understanding and support of each other's work and create the potential to influence other important public policy debates." Such views refer to new understandings and new relationships that are distinct from and transcend specific living-wage campaigns and short-term (mutual) self-interest collaboration. For example, Stephanie Luce reports that union participants saw living-wage campaigns as an opportunity "to break down stereotypes of the labor movement as monolithic" and to "humanize people's perceptions of labor" (Luce 2001, 143). A labor organizer told her that the campaign "helped us gain allies, and start dialogue with groups we never otherwise would have" (146). One union reported that it had never before worked with 90 percent of the groups that were its living-wage coalition partners (146).

These and other reports suggest a potential reconceptualization of other parties involved and also of the nature of the interorganizational and intermovement relationships. In organizers' and advocates' descriptions of the prospect of the living-wage movement, one can perceive visions of more fluid, supportive, and less easily divided cross-sector cooperation and collaboration, a closing of a great divide between labor and community in a context where each needs the other(s). Implicit in this vision is the potential for unions to address issues outside their conventional concern and for religious and community groups to effectively link their efforts to employment-based issues.

Interpreting Ordinance Adoption: Nature, Timing, Patterns, and Processes

Why Local and Why Now?

Changes in the patterns of federalism and income distributions provide insight into why the living-wage movement occurred when it did and at the level of government it did. A recurrent theme in U.S. federalism posits a pendulum effect for policy responsibility between the national and subnational levels of government. Aggressive innovations in antipoverty and income maintenance programs by the federal government in the 1960s and 1970s yielded to wholesale abandonment of these same programs or their devolution to subnational governments over the past two decades (Donahue 1997). An increasingly conservative national politics discouraged federal innovation and intervention, leaving progressive activists greater opportunities for organizing at local levels. Federal withdrawal effectively created a welfare and wage policy vacuum that shifted organizing activity to subnational government levels. The political arena for a progressive politics aimed at attacking poverty and pursuing income maintenance programs focused on the states, counties, cities, and special districts. This local policy responsibility for progressive initiatives is reminiscent of a similar response to federal abandonment of welfare policies in the 1920s, when state and local governments pioneered experimentation with unemployment compensation, social security, public employment programs, and other income maintenance measures later incorporated into the New Deal. By the 1990s, a similar shift in federalism devolved income maintenance policy responsibility to local governments.

Simultaneous with devolution of income maintenance policy, the robust economic performance of the 1990s featured increases in both wealth and poverty, where income polarization produced dramatic gains at the top and declining wages at the bottom of the wage scale. Progressive activists focused attention on low-wage workers whose relative income status declined during a decade of unprecedented prosperity. Privatization of previously publicly provided city services contributed to the decline in low-wage earnings by substituting private labor market pay decreases for previous publicly guaranteed income floors.

In the structural context of federal devolution and labor market income polarization, unions rediscovered their locals and their central labor councils (CLCs). Ness and Eimer (2001, 4) recount the development: "In 1994 these CLC leaders organized a meeting to discuss strategies for revitalizing councils, and with the ascent of the Sweeny administration in 1995, these effort(s) were given moral and material support by the national AFL-CIO." The Union Cities program followed, and labor sought alliances with religious and community organizations. Activists drawn from labor, religious, and community organizations, recognizing the shift to local policy responsibility as a political opportunity, adopted organizing strategies and formed coalitions that became the campaign for the living wage. A bottom-up strategy of grassroots organizing ensued, allowing for a progressive politics more feasible within local government jurisdictions than the increasingly conservative national politics.

Where and Why Are Ordinances Adopted?

Whereas most living-wage studies have addressed the economic impacts of ordinances, a few living-wage studies have considered the nature of the local coalitions and campaigns. We review these latter studies and generate a beginning consideration of the factors associated with the success of living-wage campaigns. We end with summary comments reflecting on the available data.

Pollin and Luce (1998) suggest that the small size of municipal polities inhibits money-dominated politics and facilitates the impact of advocacy coalitions. They also argue that urban poverty and limited low-wage employment, especially in the face of extensive public subsidies for development, create opportunity. Other scholars use urban political theory to identify the types of cities in which public subsidies are linked to redistributive measures. Fiscal and economic variables, as well as "residential need," are key factors in this perspective (Goetz 1990; Reese 1998).

Martin (2001) doubts that the key factors explaining the adoption of living-wage laws are endogenous to cities. Discounting poverty levels and similar economic factors, he argues that political resources available to local labor and community organizations matter, in interaction with national networks that provide policy models and expertise from other cities. Using a logistical regression analysis of the factors affecting whether the cities with populations of 100,000 or more have enacted living-wage laws, he finds that economic factors are not significant and that the interaction between the existence of an ACORN chapter and union density has a positive and significant effect. Martin's analysis suffers from at least two evident weaknesses. First, the presence of an ACORN chapter is highly correlated with city size, also a positive and significant factor. Thus, the effect of the ACORN variable may be spurious. Secondly, he suggests that the operative dynamic in living-wage law adoption reflects the isomorphic processes described by sociological new institutionalist theory, in which actors look to other actors for policy models in times of uncertainty and without knowing the full effects of policy options. This interpretation, although plausible, is not further supported by empirical evidence.

There are more problems with the ACORN chapter hypothesis. According to ACORN's Web site (www.livingwagecampaign.org), as of June 2003 ACORN-led coalitions have won living-wage ordinances in ten cities and have participated in another ten victories. While these testify to ACORN's impact, they are hardly enough to compellingly support an account casting them as the key medium of diffusion and success for what is now over a hundred living-wage successes.

Other scholars focusing on social movements and presenting analyses of individual cases note a number of patterns regarding the nature of successful campaigns. Nearly all living-wage successes involve coalitions that include a broad range of members drawing from labor, community, and religious groups. Reynolds (1999) suggests that the 1997 Chicago coalition is typical of many coalitions. It had seventy-eight members, including neighborhood organizations, state congressional representatives, a variety of unions, a New Party chapter, a homeless advocacy group, policy centers, the League of Women Voters, religious groups, ACORN, and the Democratic Socialists of America.

In many cases, central labor councils have been the key labor player (Luce 2001). The community groups that have been critical in initiating many campaigns are often local chapters of the ACORN and Industrial Area Foundations. In a number of cities, organizations of religious leaders concerned about local economic issues either initiated the living-wage campaign or were formed in the early stages of campaign building.

The passage of living-wage laws may reflect a diffusion process where a local or regional success legitimates the concept for nearby actors, unions, community organizations, and public officials alike. The geographic cluster of living-wage ordinances suggests a process of inspiration or imitation vis-à-vis nearby cities. For example, California (fifteen), Michigan (nine), Wisconsin (six), and New York (six) account for thirty-six successes—over a third of the total. While California may be at greater "risk" for the passage of living-wage laws due to the number of California cities and municipalities, the other three states combined with Oregon (four) account for one fourth of the total, not including three cases in New Jersey. It may be possible to model the diffusion of living-wage laws from regional origins, particularly major metropolitan cities. Many of the living-wage cities or counties are not large urban areas, and within a framework of imitative diffusion, are likely to take leads from these regional hubs.

How Campaigns Work: Coalitions

Coalitions appear to be critical to living-wage victories and, as well, to long-term success. A vast majority of successful campaigns involved a mix of community, labor, and religious organizations. Once adopted, rarely are living-wage ordinances implemented without a struggle led by a supportive coalition. Portland, Oregon, for example, effectively ignored the living-wage ordinance. Without organized monitoring groups, the legislation was not enforced (Reynolds 1999, 76).

Despite numerous successes, there are tensions inherent in coalition building. The concerns coalition partners have about each other depend in part upon whether they are small local groups or larger-scale organizations and in part upon whether they represent workers or residents or allies of those who will benefit rather than the primary beneficiaries. The tensions are also a result of the different and conflicting agendas of the allied organizations as well as the history of relations among them. Many unions do not see enough for them in the living-wage campaigns to justify serious or long-term involvement unless the campaigns are directly tied to organizing drives. Nor are the community groups always convinced of the benefits to them (Levi 2001).

For example, in Los Angeles, the CLC initiated living-wage campaigns around two large-scale projects that were receiving public subsidies: the extension of Los Angeles International Airport and the development of the Dreamworks film studio. The aim of the labor movement was to ensure living wages not only for the construction workers but also those involved in the janitorial services, concessions, and other occupations that would result from the projects; the CLC also wanted to ensure job retention for those who joined the unions. Forming a coalition with community groups and churches, the CLC took the campaign to city hall, where it succeeded in winning a living-wage ordinance and worker retention. However, it still has to ensure that contractors and vendors meet the terms.

The community groups involved often disagreed among themselves and with the unions about what protections their members would receive in employment and housing from these large-scale projects. While the unions won protections under project labor agreements, special collective bargaining agreements unique to the building trades, the poor people affected by the projects received no such binding contractual coverage. Nor were the members of the community organizations confident that labor had formed an alliance with them for the long haul. Anthony Thigpenn of AGENDA, a community organization based in south Los Angeles, argues that the labor movement has to demonstrate the strategic and not just tactical advantages of coalitions, and such a demonstration requires a comprehensive and long-term regional development plan that serves the interests of both unions and communities (as cited in Levi et al. 1998).

Unions also have their share of concerns about the community organizations and their share of internal conflicts. When the IAF or ACORN is involved from the outset, unions have assurances that there will be allies able to plan and mobilize as full partners. When no such groups exist, the unions become wary. Moreover, there are real differences of opinion among labor activists about the value of coalition politics. The internationals and the locals do not always agree about strategy. Sometimes the impetus comes from one and sometimes from the other. The AFL-CIO national, regional, and state offices add yet more layers in negotiating strategy. Even among CLCs committed to the Union Cities program with its emphasis on regional development and organizing, there is disagreement about the value of living-wage campaigns. Unions have limited resources and must consider trade-offs. Should energy and resources be put into mobilizing for living-wage campaigns or put straight into workplace organizing? When a first contract is under negotiation, should low-wage workers hold out for the higher living wage or settle for salaries lower than those mandated by a living-wage ordinance but still representative of a victory for that local?

Evaluating Living-Wage Strategy

Revisiting Prospects

In the context of the numerous living-wage successes, we can consider questions about whether the living-wage strategy is likely to deliver on the prospects for broad and enduring change. Up to this point the attention paid to the living-wage movement by progressives has been largely laudatory (although many union leaders have questioned its utility in advancing their organizational efforts and interests). Bruce Nissen's cautious judgment that "the jury is still out on how effectively unions can work with others to build 'horizontal' coalitions engaging in social movement activities" (Nissen 2000, 49) stands as an appropriate reminder that the likelihood that these prospects will be fulfilled are still unknown. Yet, as advocates, interested allies, and analysts consider the future and in some cases orient current choices around imagined future outcomes, it is important to consider critically the strengths and weaknesses of the living-wage strategy regarding both direct antipoverty and such movement-building outcomes. Does it have the potential to truly facilitate these movement-oriented possibilities? What is the likelihood that it can lay "the foundation for a long-term social movement for economic justice," as envisioned by one local campaign (Reynolds 1999, 75)? Does the living-wage movement offer the "building blocks" for a broader progressive social movement? While some theories of organizing might suggest that activating citizens is a good in itself, we suggest that this "good" should be held in tension with strategic factors. Below, we attempt to constructively examine the living-wage strategy and identify some of its limitations in relation to both antipoverty and movement-building outcomes. We identify four main limitations before revisiting the strengths of the living-wage strategy.

Limits of Living-Wage Strategies

Creates No Clear Constituency or Action Capability

It is difficult to identify who is covered by an ordinance at any particular time. Workers may move in and out of the beneficiary pool based on changes in business assistance, public contracting, their specific work assignments, or changes in the ordinances. Some reports have indicated that potential beneficiaries were not even aware of the law or its potential effects on them. This ambiguity regarding coverage is most likely a drawback over time. Ordinances do not facilitate the generation of an interested constituency aware of, benefiting from, and willing to fight for their continuation, or what Paul Pierson has referred to as "policy feedback" (Pierson 1994). It is unlikely that any publicly visible living-wage constituency will exist apart from substantial independent efforts by unions and community groups.

Furthermore, living-wage beneficiaries share no obvious action capability. Whereas unions have shared job sites and community members share a geographic concentration, living-wage beneficiaries are spread across firms and economic sectors, making collective action difficult. In the long run, this means that the living wage as a continuing organizing effort, or as a distinct source of energy and mobilization, has limited prospects.

Scope and Scale Limit Policy Reach

The living-wage issue appears limited as a vehicle to extend gains beyond the very modest ordinances. First, the structure of the ordinances themselves—certain wage floors applying to a particular subset of workers employed by private firms—means that implementation is not easily publicly verified and is dependent on active enforcement by government officials. This in turn may necessitate oversight and prodding by advocates, who also may face attempts to repeal or amend the laws. Overall, implementation of living-wage ordinances is relatively easily obfuscated and possibly eluded.

Second, the particularistic nature of the policy both fragments efforts to address economic needs and creates potential divisions within groups of workers. For example, the compromise living wage policy adopted by the New York City Council applies only to home health care workers, as other workers included in earlier proposals were notably excluded from coverage. This creates uneven and partial policies for different groups, complicating efforts to devise comprehensive and sufficient policies.

Finally, and most relevant to the unemployed, welfare recipients, and their advocates, the rhetoric of the living wage is not incompatible with a stigmatizing distinction between workers and nonworkers. The formal policies themselves offer nothing for those without jobs. One of the justifications for living-wage laws emphasizes the contradiction between working and being poor. This values working people and suggests they deserve a better status but ignores nonworkers.

Hidden Opportunity Costs

In some cases, living-wage campaigns clearly appear to have mobilized new participants, generated new resources and political opportunities, and reactivated latent human and financial resources. However, in some cities the active parties have been the "usual suspects" already largely involved in related struggles. When this occurs, living-wage campaigns may reflect a *redirection* of resources rather than the *generation* of new resources. While this redirection may be a fruitful choice, it may come at the cost of other efforts in terms of moral and political capital as well as financial and human resources.

Uncertain Outcomes for Low-Income Workers, Limited and Nonexistent Gains for Unemployed and Welfare Recipients

The actual effect of living-wage ordinances on low-income workers is not clear. Conventional economic theory suggests that as labor costs rise, some of the least qualified workers may lose jobs. The limited multicity, postordinance research conducted by David Neumark (2002) suggests this is the case. However, he also reports a slight decrease in poverty due to wage gains by the covered workers. Alternative models, and some case studies, contrastingly suggest minimal adverse employment effects. One issue is whether living wages are a better strategy for addressing poverty than other policies, such as the earned income tax credit (EITC). These uncertainties are relevant to assessments of the living-wage strategy in terms of direct wage and poverty outcomes.

Noting Additional Benefits: Weighing Potentials and Limits

Even with the limitations of the living-wage strategy, it has other qualities that stir great interest. In addition to wage and poverty effects, and the three main movement prospects discussed above, a few other features are important to note, some of which point out the flip side of living-wage strategy limitations.

- Living-wage initiatives take the offensive, set terms of debate, and require opposition energy.
- The discrete, limited nature of the living-wage framework facilitates mobilization and moral claims without requiring a "grand vision" for economic restructuring.
- Living-wage debates focus attention on the realities of low wages and the lives of the working poor.
- The public costs of living-wage ordinances are diffuse and difficult to trace, leaving little room for opponents to argue against the policy as part of an antigovernment spending platform.
- Living-wage wins keep hope alive for progressive economic policies.
- Living-wage campaigns provide a vehicle for a wide variety of individuals to exercise agency.

We offer a few questions about the utility of local living-wage campaigns as a movement-building strategy:

- Does this strategy generate new participants or primarily represent a reallocation of already busy organizers and activists?
- Does this strategy generate new resources or merely reshuffle existing resources?
- Are new relationships formed (or likely to be formed) during the effort, or are the likely participants already networked?
- Do living-wage coalitions remain active?
- Do coalitions extend gains and address other issues?
- Is the living-wage ordinance implemented? Is it monitored?
- Are the visible means by which to transfer the dialogue on living wages laterally to other issues, and upward to create more macrolevel considerations of economics, distribution, and social welfare structures?

Conclusion

In an era dominated by social conservatism, political retrenchment, and shrinking welfare provision, living-wage campaigns stand out as one of the few recent successes for progressive initiatives. Living-wage campaigns feature several distinctive characteristics that suggest a basis for successful progressive policy enactment. They are driven by bottom-up, not top-down, organizing strategies, they energize broad coalitions whose member organizations may be new to each other or reformed from prior alliances, they appeal to moral understandings of socially acceptable compensation levels for public workers, they engage the skills and energies of old and new community activists, and they create new and mobilize existing resources to surmount barriers to a progressive politics.

The impacts of the living-wage movement are multiple and not yet fully understood. The movement has changed a range of wage-setting practices and is potentially reshaping a number of related labor processes. In addition to the direct effects on workers and their families, the living-wage campaigns have raised important questions about economic and political practices and have also stimulated creative rethinking of theoretical and applied issues heatedly disputed regarding minimum wage policies (e.g., Neumark 2002). The most lasting effects, however, may be in the political sphere, in the form of new coalitions, issue framings, and public policies.

During a nationally conservative era, the living-wage movement has drawn upon the creativity and agency of local activists whose energies and skills are marshaled to a progressive politics acting upon locally defined opportunity structures. Adopting a local focus as the most promising for their campaigns, living-wage organizations and their activist leadership assemble diverse coalitions by appealing to shared sentiments and framing the living-wage issue as a moral debate over the compensation of public workers. Frequently assuming a leadership role in these coalitions, organized labor has made real its newfound pledges to revitalize locals and central labor councils while reaching out to women and people of color. Labor also has acted to organize new members and to chart innovative wage policy locally. Community and religious organizations see it in their interest to join with labor in this movement.

An important effect of these living-wage coalitions may be increased long-term cooperation and collaboration between unions and various types of community organizations. The widely shared experiences of positive local union-community relationships and, most importantly, of victories may diffuse through these respective networks and facilitate future coalitions. By building trust, raising belief in joint efficacy, and suggesting new cooperative possibilities, living-wage campaigns may lower future costs and heighten the gains from innovative coalitions and partnerships. The living-wage campaigns demonstrate that coalitions of diverse actors and organizations, while always difficult to build and fragile over time, are possible. The major significance of the living-wage movement may in fact lie in the construction of coalitions committed to attacking poverty and new strategies for improving the lives of low-wage workers.

Returning to the explicit goals and gains of the living-wage movement, a question remains. What kind of fight against poverty does the living-wage campaign represent? To the extent that it mandates a self-sustaining living standard for workers of publicly assisted firms, it represents a unique approach to attacking poverty. But in its scale, scope, and implementation it is a less effective tool than project labor agreements, EITC, or comprehensive minimum wage laws. Because they are partial to publicly assisted firms, highly variable from place to place, found in some places but not others, and lacking uniform standards and applications, the living-wage laws are limited in their power to eradicate poverty. Still, the impact of the living-wage on covered workers represents a forceful reminder of the moral principle that workers in publicly assisted firms doing the public's business should receive no less than self-sustaining compensation for their labor. And what today is limited to selected local communities may tomorrow not only be extended to public workers generally, but also provide standards for wage earners generally. A larger project expanding the scale and scope of guaranteeing for all workers a living wage can energize and inform future activists and the coalitions they lead, the working poor among their membership, and a revitalized labor movement.

Note

Funding was provided by a grant from the Russell Sage Foundation to the Harry Bridges Center for Labor Studies at the University of Washington to research the political and economic implications of living-wage campaigns. An earlier article (Levi, Olson, and Steinman 2002–2003) developed some of the themes found in this chapter, while other themes are elaborated here. For critical feedback on drafts of this chapter, we thank Margaret Levi, Stephanie Luce, and Shelly Lundberg.

References

ACORN (Association of Community Organizations for Reform Now). "ACORN and Living Wage." Introduction to ACORN's Living Wage Web site, available at www.livingwagecampaign.org (21 June 2003).

Bronfenbrenner, Kate, Sheldon Friedman, Richard W. Hurd, Rudolph A. Oswald, and Ronald L. Seeber. 1998. *Organizing to Win*. Ithaca, NY: Cornell University Press.

Champlin, Dell P., and Janet T. Knoedler. 2002. "Wages in Public Interest: Insight from Thorstein Veblen and J.M. Clark." *Journal of Economic Issues* 36, no. 4 (December): 877–92.

Chapman, Jeff. 2002. "The Living Wage Movement in 2002." MovingIdeas.org. 16 December 2002. Available at www.acorn.org/campaigns/pc.php?p=186.

Donahue, John D. 1997. *Disunited States*. New York: Basic Books.

Fine, Janice. 2001. "Community Unionism in Baltimore and Stamford: Beyond Particularism." *Working USA* 4, no. 3 (Winter): 59–85.

Goetz, Edward G. 1990. "Type II Policy and Mandated Benefits in Economic Development." *Urban Affairs Quarterly* 26, no. 2: 170–90.

Levi, Margaret, et al. 1998. "Notes on the Metro Unionism Conference." 12–14 June. University of Washington, Seattle.

———. 2001. "Capitalizing on Labor's Capital." In *Social Capital and Poor Communities*, ed. M.E. Warren et al., 246–66. New York: Russell Sage Foundation.

Levi, Margaret, and Gillian Hughes Murphy. 2003. "Battling for Global Justice: Protests Against the WTO in Seattle." *The Encyclopedia of American Social Movements*, ed. Immanuel Ness. Armonk, NY: M.E. Sharpe.

Levi, Margaret, and David Olson. 2000. "The Battles in Seattle." *Politics and Society* 28, no. 3: 217–37.

Levi, Margaret, David J. Olson and Erich Steinman. 2002–03. "Living-Wage Campaigns and Laws." *Working USA* 6, no. 3 (Winter): 111–32.

Lipsky, Michael, and Margaret Levi. 1972. "Community Organization as a Political Resource." In *People and Politics in Urban Society*, ed. Harlan Hahn, 175–99. Beverly Hills, CA: Sage.

Luce, Stephanie. 2001. "Building Political Power and Community Coalitions: The Role of Central Labor Councils in the Living Wage Movement." In *Central Labor Councils and the Revival of American Unionism*, ed. Immanuel Ness and Stuart Eimer. Armonk, NY: M.E. Sharpe.

McAdam, Doug. 1982. *Political Process and the Development of Black Insurgency*. Chicago: University of Chicago Press.

Martin, Isaac. 2001. "Dawn of the Living Wage—The Diffusion of a Redistributive Municipal Policy." *Urban Affairs Review* 36, no. 4 (March): 470–96.

Ness, Immanuel, and Stuart Eimer. 2001. *Central Labor Councils and the Revival of American Unionism*. Armonk, NY: M.E. Sharpe.

Neumark, David. 2002. *How Living Wage Laws Affect Low-Wage Workers and Low-Income Families*. San Francisco: Public Policy Institute of California.

Nissen, Bruce. 1999. *The Impact of a Living Wage Ordinance on Miami-Dade County*. Miami: Florida International University Press.

———. 2000. "Living-Wage Campaigns from a 'Social Movement' Perspective: The Case of Miami." *Labor Studies Journal* 25, no. 3 (Fall): 29–50.

Pierson, Paul. 1994. *Dismantling the Welfare State? Reagan, Thatcher, and the Politics of Retrenchment*. Cambridge, England, and New York: Cambridge University Press.

Pollin, Robert, and Stephanie Luce. 1998. *The Living Wage: Building a Fair Economy*. New York: New Press (distributed by W.W. Norton).

Reese, Laura A. 1998. "Sharing the Benefits of Economic Development: What Cities Use Type II Policies?" *Urban Affairs Review* 33, no. 5 (May): 686–711.

Reynolds, David. 1999. "The Living Wage Movement Sweeps the Nation." *Working USA* 3, no. 3 (September/October): 61–80.

Voss, Kim, and Rachel Sherman. 2000. "Breaking the Iron Law of Oligarchy: Union Revitalization in the American Labor Movement." *American Journal of Sociology* 106, no. 2 (September): 303–49.

Zabin, Carol, and Isaac Martin. 1999. "Living-Wage Campaigns in the Economic Policy Arena: Four Case Studies from California." A report for The Phoenix Fund for Workers and Communities, The New World Foundation. Available at www.phoenixfund.org (June 1999).

9

Labor-Welfare Linkages and the Imperative of Organizing Low-Wage Women Workers

Louise Simmons

For many low-income women, the last decade has been a nightmare. Welfare reform in 1996 heralded a new punitive era characterized by the dreadful realities of low-wage work, a shredded safety net, and conflicting social policies—all of which look to continue into the foreseeable future. Many middle-class women struggle with the balance between work and family and are supportive of policies that address these tensions. They may even be encouraged to take time off from work when they have children. Yet poor women are mandated into the workforce and now being asked to work longer hours in order to comply with requirements for meager public assistance. As popular columnist Ellen Goodman (2002) observed, "We value mothering when the family has a paycheck-earning father. We devalue it as rapidly as a dot-com stock when [the mother] is single and poor."

In the legislative struggle over reauthorization of Temporary Assistance to Needy Families (TANF), it has been difficult to get many policy makers in Washington to hear the abundant voices of those who had endured hardships under TANF or to heed the many reports that offer criticism of TANF and the impact of welfare reform. Public officials instead seem content to showcase a number of so-called welfare success stories as justification for forging ahead with yet another cycle of policies that will keep welfare rolls low, but not end poverty. Thus, as former welfare recipients increasingly join the ranks of low-wage workers, the labor movement faces any number of opportunities and challenges in organizing, policy advocacy, and the larger social mission of labor.

Scaling Back the Social Welfare State: Class, Race, and Gender

Frances Fox Piven has argued prolifically and eloquently in this volume and elsewhere (see, for example, Piven 2002, 1998, 1997; Piven and Sampson 2001) that in this era of dramatic changes to welfare policy, welfare programs have been attacked as part of an aggressive politics of class on the part of business interests intent on reducing social welfare programs in order to discipline labor and shore up profits. Although scaling back the social welfare state is often posed as an answer to global competition, Piven argues that this option is not an inevitable or inescapable choice. Rather, this option is based on the triumph of the politics of greed and weak popular opposition in the United States. This weakness involves fragmented party structures, a struggling labor movement, an acceptance of neoliberal ideology, and "a popular culture deeply infused with racism and with sexual obsessions, as the debate over welfare showed once again" (2001, 28).

Many have observed the gender bias inherent in welfare policy (see Abramovitz 1996, 2002; Gordon 1994, 2002). Others have documented the distinctly racialized aspects of welfare reform: support for policy changes came from some quarters on the basis of racial stereotypes and popular misconceptions about the behavior of poor women of color, mainly African-Americans. Moreover, welfare reform has rendered some particularly severe impacts on recipients of color: there is evidence that women of color get different treatment and suffer more sanctions, family cap restrictions, and other forms of discrimination in welfare programs than white recipients (Neubeck and Cazenave 2001; Neubeck 2002). Immigrants, including many who are people of color, have also suffered inordinately under TANF. While the focus in this chapter is on aspects of welfare most relevant to the labor movement, the gender and racial issues surrounding welfare policy are also ripe for scrutiny, given how much attention and resources have been devoted to the behavior of poor women, as embodied in the marriage-promotion programs to be paid for with public funds. The very forces who want less government intervention in the market are eager to insert themselves into the personal decisions of poor women, as their lives now seem to be deemed affairs of state.

The Contours of the New Welfare Regime

The TANF program, which was established in 1996 and replaced Aid to Families with Dependent Children (AFDC), has produced a wide mixture of results. Since one feature is that each state and U.S. territory has broad discretion to design its own version of TANF, results vary from state to state and even within regions of states, depending upon specific local features. Some states employ extensive sanction systems that reduce benefits as punishment for noncompliance. While federal lifetime limits of sixty months of assistance were established within the legislation, many states have shorter time limits. States meet federal work requirements in a variety of ways. Some provide options for education and training, while other states severely limit these options and embrace a "work first" approach. Some states have established "community service" jobs, that is, workfare, while others do not rely as extensively on these alternatives. Few states are providing adequate supportive services such as child care or transportation subsidies. Federal funds that are supposed to be directed to TANF programs sometimes are used by state governments to fund other services, especially in times of budget crises. States also may privatize certain welfare functions, thus laying off public workers and also injecting the profit motive into the provision of services to some of the nation's neediest citizens. Under these arrangements, recipients may not be counseled about programs for which they are eligible. Given all of this, getting a handle on the impact of welfare reform is complex and challenging, and an entire industry has blossomed to evaluate welfare reform and assess its impact in state after state.

Research on how "welfare leavers" are faring has not given many welfare rights activists cause for optimism. The huge reduction in welfare rolls during the late 1990s has not necessarily correlated with a reduction in poverty of the former recipients. Results vary widely and so-called success stories—depictions of recipients who have found jobs and become "self-sufficient"—often correlate with the education and skill levels of the recipients. But even more importantly, the definition of the success, itself, must be scrutinized. Sanford Schram and Joe Soss (2002; see also Schram 1995) argue convincingly that the manner in which the "problem" of welfare has been defined—the issue framing, the symbolism attached to the issue, the academic research, and the policy prescriptions—has led to a very limited scope within which to both envision policy options for and evaluate the outcomes of welfare reform.

Welfare reform policy has been framed around the goals of decreasing the use of public assistance and changing the behavior of the poor. Hence, caseload reduction and employment among welfare leavers have become the criteria for success. Schram and Soss note, "Compared to improving material conditions in poor communities, it is relatively easy to pare the welfare rolls and push the poor into low-wage work" (2002, 65). Reducing poverty and inequality, creating jobs for the poor, raising low wages to lift low-wage workers out of poverty, reducing social marginality, providing assistance equitably across race and gender—these issues have not been framed as the policy goals around which to evaluate the success of welfare reform. Nor has attention been paid to waste, private sector profiteering, problems of program administration, or the dilemma of clients not gaining access to programs and entitlements for which they are eligible (Schram and Soss 2002).

Even within assessments of TANF that do concentrate on caseload reduction and employment of welfare recipients, a number of respected researchers highlight the problems of those who are least able to make the transition off of welfare. For example, Pamela Loprest, writing for the Urban Institute, has analyzed outcomes of families in a national sample who were involved with the welfare system. She states:

> Many former recipients who have gone to work are having difficulty making ends meet, faced with low wages and few benefits. Others returned to the welfare rolls quickly after losing a job or having child care arrangements fall through. Still other recipients have not yet joined the workforce because of multiple serious barriers that impede the transition. Some of these recipients continue to rely on welfare, and face time limits on benefits. Finally, some former welfare recipients no longer collect benefits because they failed to comply with program rules, but have few alternative sources of income. (2002, 17)

Robert Moffitt of the Brookings Institution echoes these concerns. He notes that employment rates among single mothers have increased dramatically, due in part to the strong economy of the late 1990s. However, he cautions that incomes of women leaving welfare are only slightly higher than when they received assistance and that "there is a significant group of very disadvantaged women, many no longer on welfare, who have major difficulties with employment because of poor job skills, poor physical and mental health, and other problems. Special policies also need to be directed toward this group" (2002, 1).

Transitioning to the Low-Wage Workforce

A myriad of issues confront welfare recipients in the transition to work. The issue of low wages is certainly paramount. Randy Albelda (2002) summarizes a common finding among the numerous impact studies: "What is astonishing about the results from these 'leaver' studies is how similar they are, despite the supposed diversity of programs adopted by the states. Between two-thirds and three-quarters of adults are employed most often for about 35 hours a week, earning an average hourly wage of about $7.50 in jobs that as often as not do not have health care benefits, rarely provide any sick days, and offer little or no vacation time" (79). Researchers at the Economic Policy Institute have issued several reports that examine the nature of the hardship these women face in the workforce. Heather Boushey (2001) warns that the recession of 2001 has had severe impacts in those employment sectors in which welfare recipients have been finding jobs, such as retail trade, eating and drinking establishments, the hospitality industry, and other mainly service sector jobs. Boushey and Gundersen (2001) also document the problems recent welfare recipients face, which not surprisingly include food insecurity, housing problems, health care issues, and inadequate child care. Boushey (2002a) additionally shows that even those with full-time employment experience these hardships.

In this context, hundreds of thousands of single mothers are entering the workforce to face low wages, little opportunity for advancement, and most certainly increased family stress under current welfare policies. Several research projects suggest that these single mothers transitioning from welfare, the very women who most desperately need flexible employment arrangements in order to accommodate family demands and stay employed, are not likely to have jobs that offer the necessary flexible options in order to balance work and family. For example, Harvard researchers S. Jody Heymann and Alison Earle found that mothers leaving welfare for work have less paid leave (i.e., vacation and sick time) and other kinds of flexibility in their jobs than mothers who had never been on AFDC. They tend to have jobs that lack benefits and are at greater risk of losing their jobs if they take time off to tend to the health needs of their children. They face awful choices in dealing with their children's illnesses: "They can send sick children to school, leave them home alone, leave them in the care of other children, or take unpaid leave. For parents earning close to the minimum wage, as is the case with many families exiting welfare for work, taking unpaid leave can drop the family income below the poverty level" (1999, 504).

The problems confronting low-income working families are described by Dodson, Manuel, and Bravo as the "entrenched mismatch between the imperatives of raising families and keeping jobs in low-income America" (2002, 1), producing intractable conflicts between the safety, survival, and education of children and parents' ability to maintain employment. Many parents experience job loss, discipline, denied wages, and other problems when they require time off to meet family needs. Both this study and Heymann and Earle's (1999) work cite the enormous difficulty for parents in low-income families of devoting adequate time and attention to children, especially when the children have learning disabilities or chronic health needs.

Flexibility in employment schedules is clearly beneficial to low-wage women workers, yet according to Elaine McCrate (2002), there are gender and racial dimensions to work schedule flexibility. Single mothers have particularly rigid schedules, and African-American workers are much less likely than white workers to exercise discretion over scheduling. Individuals in supervisory positions or policy-making authority and those in higher-paying jobs enjoy greater flexibility than other workers. McCrate advocates family-supportive public policy such as legislating a minimum number of sick and personal days and vacation time so that workers can utilize this time to meet family needs. She further suggests that vigorously enforced affirmative action and unionization can assist women and black workers in gaining more flexible jobs.

Boushey points out that welfare recipients who leave welfare and maintain employment have the best chance of real wage growth over time. The chances of keeping a job increase significantly with several factors: available, consistent, formal (center-based), and affordable and subsidized child care arrangements; job quality, including employer-provided health insurance; and higher starting wages. In her research, those women who had these advantages were significantly more likely to be employed after two years than those without. For example:

- Former welfare recipients with young children who use formal day care are nearly three times as likely to be employed after two years as those who do not.
- Former welfare recipients who receive employer-provided health

insurance are 2.6 times as likely to still be employed after three years as those who do not.

- Former welfare recipients who started their jobs earning in the second to bottom quintile are 63 percent more likely to still be employed after two years as those who started in the bottom quintile (Boushey 2002b, 2).

Boushey suggests that rather than adopting "work first" approaches to job placement for welfare recipients, better quality jobs should be promoted and employers should be helped in offering health insurance. Moreover, policies need to be adopted that improve starting wages through such measures as "raising the minimum wage and fostering the development of unions in low-wage sectors of the economy" (3).

The Benefits of Organizing

It is thus becoming apparent to former welfare recipients and many advocates that high on the list of strategies to challenge this bleak picture and create any sense of hope is unionization. Although a vast range of policies and action must be undertaken to truly provide individuals in the welfare system with options to better their lives, successfully organizing into a union or being hired at a unionized work site offers greater likelihood for higher wages and more control and dignity on the job. Consider the Bureau of Labor Statistics numbers cited in Sklar, Mykyta, and Wefald that compare median weekly pay for full-time workers by union affiliation in 2000:

- Union members' (all races, both genders) median earnings were $696 compared to $542 for nonunion workers.
- Unionized women workers' median earnings were $616 compared to $472 for nonunion women workers.
- For African-Americans, median weekly earnings for those who were union members were $596 compared to $436 for nonunion members; for African-American women, the respective median earnings were $564 compared to $408; for African-American men, $619 compared to $479.
- For Hispanics, median weekly earnings for those who were union members were $584 compared to $377 for nonunion members; for Hispanic women, the respective median earnings were $489 com-

pared to $346; for Hispanic men, $631 compared to $394. (Sklar, Mykyta, and Wefald 2001, 151)

The yearly impact of these patterns means thousands of dollars more in income for union members. Similar patterns hold for 2001 (Bureau of Labor Statistics 2002).

Industries in which welfare recipients find work may or may not be highly unionized. However, one industry in which women leaving welfare may find employment, the retail food industry, was recently analyzed by researchers at the Institute for Women's Policy Research (IWPR). The study was sponsored by the United Food and Commercial Workers International Union and utilized Current Population Survey data to examine how unionization benefits retail food industry workers. Lovell, Song, and Shaw found that "workers in the retail food industry who are union members have significantly higher wages, higher rates of health insurance coverage, larger employment-based contributions to health insurance premiums, and higher rates of union pension coverage than nonunionized workers. Full-time and part-time workers, women and single mothers in the retail food industry all benefit from union membership" (2002, vi). The "union wage premium" for the entire industry was 31 percent, while for part-timers it was 33 percent, and for cashiers, a job category held in large numbers by women, it was a mammoth 52 percent. While these outcomes are not surprising to those associated with the labor movement, the welfare rights community has not often emphasized the benefits of unionization in its policy advocacy. Reports such as this one conducted by IWPR need to be given attention in the welfare rights arena.

However, a very small percentage of the total full-time U.S. workforce actually is in unions—under 14 percent, and an even smaller percentage of part-time workers—less than 7 percent (a group that includes large numbers of former welfare recipients) (Bureau of Labor Statistics 2002). The benefits of unionization are therefore elusive for former welfare recipients, who are blending into the low-wage unorganized workforce and desperately need to be organized.

The Labor-Welfare Nexus

The imperative of reaching and organizing these workers fits within the discussion of how to strengthen and build the labor movement. Many ideas are circulating about this most urgent of all challenges for labor. For example, Richard Freeman and Joel Rogers (2002) advocate what they refer to as "open source unionism" as a strategy to build the labor movement. This approach envisions extending a new form of union membership to workers beyond those work sites in which unions have demonstrated majority support and where collective bargaining agreements have been negotiated. Making use of the Internet, this form of unionism would encompass a new range of activities by which workers with workplace problems could gain assistance, information, and referrals. Other methods could be developed to extend unionism to workers who currently do not have a mechanism to share its benefits. More interaction with community forces could be part of this model, especially political action, as membership is redefined. Open source unionism is meant to complement existing forms of union membership within the U.S. system of labor relations.

Clearly, if there was ever a group of workers who could benefit from such new forms of union membership, it is the low-wage unorganized—or not-yet-organized—workforce, which includes many former welfare recipients. Open source unionism could address the myriad problems they encounter as they enter the workforce, particularly their rights on the job, supportive services, and unemployment issues.

When welfare reform had just been enacted, Bill Fletcher implored the labor movement to embrace welfare recipients as members of the working class, part of labor's constituency beyond those already in unions: "This means a fight for workers' rights and economic justice, not solely a fight for an improved collective-bargaining agreement" (1997, 129). Foreshadowing some of the Freeman-Rogers argument, his comments continue to be apropos as he observed that new forms of organization would be necessary if labor is to "become the overarching voice for that larger community of workers who are seeking economic and social justice" (30), including councils of unemployed and underemployed, labor-led economic development projects, cooperatives, and other associations.

Much is at stake for labor as welfare policy continues to evolve in the TANF reauthorization process and beyond. I have observed elsewhere (Simmons 2002) that instituting TANF as a time limited program, with broad discretion by states, has done general harm to the entire scope of the welfare state. The creation of workfare programs, the privatization of welfare services, the expansion of the low-wage workforce, and the shredding of the safety net harm all workers, not simply those who spend some portion of their lives on public assistance. But there are ways to address these issues, and there are examples of labor's meaningful involvement in the struggle over welfare programs and the plight of low-wage workers that can be replicated and adapted to local conditions and local communities.

From labor's standpoint, community unionism (see Fine 2001) as embodied in projects like the Los Angeles Alliance for a New Economy (LAANE), Working Partnerships in San Jose, and BUILD in Baltimore is a vehicle that helps frame and develop organizing in innovative ways. In Connecticut, a recently established organizing and policy advocacy group, the Connecticut Center for a New Economy (CCNE), that takes LAANE as its inspiration, is also attempting to address the problems of low-wage workers. Through a combination of labor and community organizing, advocacy and research, CCNE advances an agenda that suggests (at least) three options to raise income for these workers: raising and enforcing minimum wage or living-wage standards; investing in training and education; and nurturing collective bargaining (CCNE 2001). Through support of union organizing drives and progressive public policy, CCNE is attempting to build a movement that transforms low-wage jobs into family-sustaining employment.

Certainly living-wage campaigns and raising the minimum wage are important parts of the picture. Living-wage coalitions have been able to get local ordinances passed in over eighty cities (and counting) (see Olson and Steinman's chapter in this volume, and Reynolds and Kern 2002). Moreover, the sophisticated tool of self-sufficiency standards (Pearce 2002) that actually measures the cost of living for different family types in different locations gives added force to the claims of these movements and can be used to verify the need for higher wages. These efforts, which can involve alliances of community, labor, and welfare rights activists, underscore the need for public policy to address low-wage work. Further, the entire arena of economic development policy is being reframed in order to elevate issues of living wages and demand that if tax incentives are offered to corporations, they make good on promises to produce jobs paying decent wages. An exciting conference in July 2002, "Reclaiming Economic Development," sponsored by Good Jobs First, brought together several hundred activists from around the country to construct a progressive economic development agenda that addresses poverty and creates opportunity. The needs of former welfare recipients in the low-wage workforce certainly fit within this agenda.

In various communities, labor has been undertaking projects that benefit welfare recipients in terms of training and services. Brian Turner (2001) elaborates examples of how unions are reaching out to low-wage workers, including former welfare recipients, to provide access to job training programs that place participants into union jobs. His impressive list includes the Milwaukee Jobs Initiative, Hotel Employees and Restaurant Employees (HERE) training programs, a child care worker training program of 1199C-AFSCME (American Federation of State, County and Municipal Employees) in Philadelphia, training and placement programs in health care by 1199 in New York (part of Service Employees International Union [SEIU]), and also several examples of training programs run by the building trades in various locales. At the "Reclaiming Economic Development" conference in July 2002, speakers included representatives from the Alameda Corridor Jobs Coalition, a project in the Los Angeles area that has organized and obtained training and living-wage jobs for hundreds of individuals from communities along the Alameda Corridor, including 190 former welfare recipients, and also from Trade Unions and Residents for Apprenticeship Development and Economic Success (TRADES), a New York City organization formed by the Laborers Union that works with public housing residents who are mandated to do community service in their housing developments. So in some places, promising alliances are developing between welfare rights activists and the labor movement to meet immediate needs of former recipients, now largely low-wage workers.

Public policy advocacy is another arena for collaboration. Space limitations do not permit a full discussion of this aspect of the labor-welfare linkage, but briefly, on the national level, through the work of unions such as AFSCME, SEIU, and the AFL-CIO, and in many state and local struggles over welfare, labor, and welfare groups have been and can be essential partners in many battles. In statewide coalitions such as Working Massachusetts, the process of crafting a joint agenda allows welfare rights activists and union representatives to reach deeper levels of understanding and define new ways to work together.

By targeting low-wage women workers for organizing and creating new forms of union membership, labor can help solve the grave problems these women face and simultaneously increase the ranks of unions. Women workers are ready to be organized, as demonstrated repeatedly in recent years. The 75,000 home care workers who voted to join SEIU in 1999—the largest organizing victory in decades, and the janitors', hotel workers', and textile workers' recent organizing victories (Turner 2001) demonstrate clearly that women workers are ready to organize, even against great odds. The leadership positions that women, particularly women of color, are assuming in the labor movement—for example, Maria Elena Durazo and Goeconda Arguello-Kline within HERE (Snedeker 2002)—are also testament to women's willingness to act and capacity for leadership.

Joining unions will not eliminate all of the anguish that women leaving welfare and entering the low-wage workforce endure in dealing with housing, medical problems, child rearing, and the stress that low-income life engenders. However, it can be a critical element in women's ability to increase their incomes and assert their rights on the job.

Deepak Bhargava (2002), director of the National Campaign for Jobs and Income Support, a coalition of over 200 organizations that has been organizing on TANF reauthorization and related issues, asserts that the allies of grassroots antipoverty organizations—the religious community, labor, civil rights, women's rights, students, and other groups—are essential for any successful outcomes in struggles over poverty issues. How these allies converge with grassroots organizations led by low-income people is an open question that cannot be scripted, but Bhargava postulates that we could be facing "a turning point when crucial new ideas, frames, organizing approaches and alliances [will be] created" (208).

Perhaps one of the most important organizing approaches of all is one that is not so new, but ready to be tried by a new group of workers, the type of organizing that oppressed and exploited workers have turned to throughout modern history—organizing into unions. In so doing, low-wage women workers, some who have been on public assistance and some who have not, can begin to reclaim the power, dignity, and respect that they so profoundly deserve.

References

Abramovitz, Mimi. 1996. *Under Attack, Fighting Back: Women and Welfare in the United States.* New York: Monthly Review Press.
———. 2002. "Learning from the History of Poor and Working-Class Women's Activism." In *Lost Ground*, ed. Randy Albelda and Ann Withorn, 163–78. Cambridge, MA: South End Press.

Albelda, Randy. 2002 "Fallacies of Welfare-to-Work Policies." In *Lost Ground*, ed. Randy Albelda and Ann Withorn, 79–94. Cambridge, MA: South End Press.

Bhargava, Deepak. 2002. "Progressive Organizing on Welfare Policy." In *From Poverty to Punishment: How Welfare Reform Punishes the Poor*, ed. Gary Delgado, 199–208. Oakland, CA: Applied Research Center.

Boushey, Heather. 2001 "Last Hired, First Fired: Job Losses Plague Former TANF Recipients." EPI Issue Brief #171. Washington, DC: Economic Policy Institute. Available at http://epinet.org.

Boushey, Heather, and Bethney Gundersen. 2001. "When Work Just Isn't Enough: Measuring Hardships Faced by Families After Moving From Welfare to Work." Briefing paper. Washington, DC: Economic Policy Institute. Available at http://epinet.org.

———. 2002a. "Former Welfare Families Need More Help: Hardships Await Those Making Transition to Workforce." Briefing paper. Washington, DC: Economic Policy Institute. Available at http://epinet.org.

———. 2002b. "Staying Employed After Welfare: Work Supports and Job Quality Vital to Employment Tenure and Wage Growth." Briefing paper. Washington, DC: Economic Policy Institute. Available at http://epinet.org.

Bureau of Labor Statistics. 2002. "Median Weekly Earnings of Full-time Wage and Salary Workers by Union Affiliation and Selected Characteristics." Available at http://stats.bls.gov/news.release/union2.t02.htm.

Connecticut Center for a New Economy (CCNE). 2001. *Good Jobs, Strong Communities: Creating a High-Wage Future for Connecticut.* New Haven: Connecticut Center for a New Economy. Available at www.ctneweconomy.org.

Dodson, Lisa, Tiffany Manuel, and Ellen Bravo. 2002. *Keeping Jobs and Raising Families in Low-Income America: It Just Doesn't Work.* A Report of the Across the Boundaries Project, Radcliffe Public Policy Center, and 9 to 5 National Association of Working Women. Cambridge, MA: Radcliffe Institute for Advanced Study, Harvard University. Available at www.radcliffe.edu/pubpol.

Fine, Janice. 2001. "Community Unionism in Baltimore and Stamford: Beyond the Politics of Particularism." *Working USA* 4, no. 3: 59–85.

Fletcher, Bill, Jr. 1997. "Seizing the Time Because the Time Is Now: Welfare Repeal and Labor Reconstruction." In *Audacious Democracy: Labor, Intellectuals, and the Social Reconstruction of America*, ed. Steven Fraser and Joshua Freeman, 119–31. New York: Houghton Mifflin Mariner Books.

Freeman, Richard, and Joel Rogers. 2002. "Open Source Unionism: Beyond Exclusive Collective Bargaining," *Working USA* 5, no. 4: 8–40.

Goodman, Ellen. 2002. "The Working Mom Con." *The Boston Globe*, 23 May, A19.

Gordon, Linda. 1994. *Pitied but Not Entitled: Single Mothers and the History of Welfare.* New York: Free Press.

———. 2002. "Who Deserves Help? Who Must Provide?" In *Lost Ground*, ed. Randy Albelda and Ann Withorn, 9–25. Cambridge, MA: South End Press.

Heymann, S. Jody, and Alison Earle. 1999. "The Impact of Welfare Reform on Parents' Ability to Care for Their Children's Health." *American Journal of Public Health* 89, no. 4: 502–5.

Loprest, Pamela. 2002. "Making the Transition from Welfare to Work: Successes but Continuing Concerns." In *Welfare Reform: The Next Act*, ed. Alan Weil and Kenneth Finegold, 17–31. Washington, DC: The Urban Institute Press.

Lovell, Vicky, Xue Song, and April Shaw. 2002. *The Benefits of Unionization for Workers in the Retail Food Industry.* Washington, DC: Institute for Women's Policy Research. Available at www.iwpr.org.

McCrate, Elaine. 2002. "Working Mothers in a Double Bind: Working Moms, Minorities Have the Most Rigid Schedules, and Are Paid Less for the Sacrifice." Briefing paper. Washington, DC: Economic Policy Institute. Available at http://epinet.org.

Moffitt, Robert. 2002. "From Welfare to Work: What the Evidence Shows." Brookings Institution Policy Brief No. 13, January 2002. Available at http://www.brookings.edu.

Neubeck, Kenneth. 2002. "Attacking Welfare Racism/Honoring Poor People's Human Rights." In *Lost Ground*, ed. Randy Albelda and Ann Withorn, 113–27. Cambridge, MA: South End Press.

Neubeck, Kenneth, and Noel Cazenave. 2001. *Welfare Racism: Playing the Race Card Against America's Poor.* New York: Routledge.

Pearce, Diana. 2002. "Measuring Welfare Reform Success by a Different Standard." In *From Poverty to Punishment: How Welfare Reform Punishes the Poor*, ed. Gary Delgado, 166–86. Oakland, CA: Applied Research Center.

Piven, Frances Fox. 1997. "The New Reserve Army of Labor." In *Audacious Democracy: Labor, Intellectuals, and the Social Reconstruction of America*, ed. Steven Fraser and Joshua Freeman, 106–18. New York: Houghton Mifflin Mariner Books.

———. 1998. "Welfare and Work." *Social Justice* 25, no. 1: 67–82.

———. 2002. "Globalization, American Politics, and Welfare Policy." In *Lost Ground*, ed. Randy Albelda and Ann Withorn, 27–41. Cambridge, MA: South End Press.

Piven, Frances Fox, and Tim Sampson. 2001. "Welfare: What Is to Be." *Social Policy* 32, no. 1: 40–44.

Reynolds, David, and Jen Kern. 2002. "Labor and the Living Wage Movement." *Working USA* 5, no. 3: 17–45.

Schram, Sanford. 1995. *Words of Welfare: The Poverty of Social Science and the Social Science of Poverty.* Minneapolis: University of Minnesota Press.

Schram, Sanford, and Joe Soss. 2002. "Success Stories: Welfare Reform, Policy Discourse, and the Politics of Research." In *Lost Ground*, ed. Randy Albelda and Ann Withorn, 57–78. Cambridge, MA: South End Press.

Simmons, Louise. 2002. "Unions and Welfare Reform: Labor's Stake in the On-Going Struggle Over the Welfare State." *Labor Studies Journal* 27, no. 2: 65–83.

Sklar, Holly, Laryssa Mykyta, and Susan Wefald. 2001. *Raise the Floor: Wages and Policies That Work for All of Us.* New York: Ms. Foundation for Women.

Snedeker, Lisa. 2002. "Hispanic Women Rising in Ranks of Labor Movement." *Hartford Courant*, 1 July, E1–2.

Turner, Brian. 2001. "Union Innovations: Moving Workers from Poverty Into Family-Sustaining Jobs." In *Low Wage Workers in the New Economy,* ed. Richard Kazis and Marc Miller, 347–62. Washington, DC: Urban Institute Press.

10

Urban Poverty, Social Welfare, and Human Rights

James Jennings

This collection of readings is an opportunity to propose that the idea of social justice should be reintroduced in civic dialogues and debates about the future of our cities and social policies in the areas of housing, health, community development, and public safety. It is proposed that the standard of living at the local level for all people cannot be improved without social policies and accompanying politics that seek to manage and redistribute wealth equitably. Furthermore, the notion that social and taxation policies affecting poor people and labor should be based on the subsidization of corporate wealth in society is economically inefficient in terms of improving the overall social and economic health of U.S. society. Social justice and human rights as an idea and clarion call for building progressive and effective public policies have been pushed off the table of political debate. This is a serious matter because certain kinds of issues and related questions about public policy are not considered by decision makers or citizens when the call for social justice becomes irrelevant, inefficient, or even unpatriotic. Many people are concerned about inequality and deteriorating living conditions in cities and neighborhoods. Infusing this concern with a call for social justice generates a framework that challenges the dominant civic and political framework based on continual concentration of corporate wealth and the militarization of U.S. society. Only by developing a politics and public policies based on social justice can we respond effectively to problems such as continuing racial and ethnic divisions, persistent poverty, growing economic inequality and insecurity, and an increasingly unaccountable military and prison-industrial state.

I am proposing that social justice has to be reintroduced in our civic dialogues, as is suggested in the earlier chapters of this book. This concept is necessary in helping the nation resolve some of our most intractable social and economic problems. Doing the right thing, challenging inequality, and expanding our economic democracy, and not being defensive about calls for social justice, can be an effective tool for moving neighborhoods and cities forward in positive ways. A lens of social justice and respect for human rights can help us to raise the questions appropriate for responding to persistent poverty, racial and ethnic divisions, and economic distress. A civic framework reflecting strong support for social justice is ultimately the most efficient and effective way to help our cities and neighborhoods and bring people together to work on collective social and economic benefits.

Continuing and Intensifying Social Contrasts

This is a timely discussion because we are living in the midst of social contrasts that raise issues and doubts regarding our national commitment to civil and human rights for all Americans. These contrasts raise moral and economic issues. Our society is characterized by divisions between people who eat well and people needing food stamps in order to eat; people who have homes and people who are homeless; children who have bright futures and children who can only grow alienated; people who enjoy economic security and people who live in economic desperation; people who have access to health care, and people who cannot afford to get ill.[1] These kinds of contrasts are not new and actually represent a basic feature of the history of the United States. As noted by W.E.B. DuBois in his commencement address to the graduates of Fisk University in 1938:

> The most distressing fact in the present world is poverty; not absolute poverty, because some folk are rich and many are well-to-do, not poverty as great as some lands and other historical ages have known; but poverty more poignant and discouraging because it comes after a dream of wealth; of riotous, wasteful and even vulgar accumulation of individual riches, which suddenly leaves the majority of mankind today without enough to eat; without proper shelter; and without sufficient clothing. (DuBois 1970, 170)

A major difference between DuBois's description of an earlier period and the current period is that inequality between rich and poor has become wider although vaster wealth has been created than could have ever been imagined. Dr. Martin Luther King Jr. voiced similar concerns about the issue of poverty in the midst of vast wealth. King's vision of social justice led him to call for economic democracy where poor people, and working-class people, could enjoy the fruits of their contributions to the building and concentration of massive wealth in this country. This is why he sought to lead a multiracial poor people's march on Washington, D.C., a few months before his assassination in 1968.

Both thinkers focused on these kinds of contrasts as a result of their beliefs that it is poor people, the working-class, and for hundreds of years black slaves, who played a major role in building this nation's enormous wealth. Given this history, there is no moral, political, or even economic justification for the lopsided concentration of wealth in the United States today while those who provided the basis for the creation of wealth remain poor or near-poor. These contrasts represent a moral crisis because problems associated with poverty and inequality occur in the midst of the richest and most powerful nation today. They also represent an economic crisis because public policies that simply serve to make the rich richer are inefficient and ineffective in responding to the economic needs of the nation.

These unnecessary contrasts are reflected in many problems facing cities and neighborhoods. In 2002, for example, the city of Hartford, Connecticut, was the subject of a *New York Times* story that reported significant differences between haves and have-nots. The article appropriately titled, "Poverty in a Land of Plenty: Can Hartford Ever Recover?" noted that almost a third of the residents of this city are impoverished while living in the wealthiest state in the nation (Zielbauer 2002). The article reminded the reader of similar problems found in most large cities, including continuing racial and ethnic divisions (while racial and ethnic diversity is increasing), persistent poverty, economic insecurity for many, deteriorating physical infrastructures, and inadequate housing and public health systems.

Increasing wealth inequality has not, and cannot, solve these kinds of problems. There are widening economic gaps between poor people, working-class people, middle-class people, and the rich. Over the last several years, the after-tax income has increased considerably while that of low-income Americans has declined. Poor people have become poorer while the rich have become superrich. In 1970 a family on AFDC (Assistance to Families with Dependent Children) received a grant that was equal to 66 percent of the official poverty level; by 1991 that same family received but 41 percent of the official poverty level. This percentage has continued to decline into the late 1990s (see Jennings 1994). Numerous studies have documented how poor and working-class people subsidize wealthy people. This has occurred through a deterioration of real wages over the last several decades and a lessening of tax burdens on corporate and other rich sectors of society (Palley 2000). As a result of policies biased toward the rich (versus biased on behalf of the hard work more associated with poor and working-class people), the richest Americans have accumulated enormously large proportions of the wealth produced in U.S. society.

The burden of subsidizing the rich that falls on the poor and working-class people has increased under the administration of President Bush. In 2001 he pushed successfully, with both Republican and Democratic support, a $1.3 trillion tax cut over ten years that has not done anything to increase economic productivity or benefits to Americans. According to Citizens for Tax Justice, this tax cut means that in 2003 the richest "top 1% will get more than $30,000 each on average; a family at the median level of income will get about $289; and a family at the bottom fifth of income, making an average of $9,900 a year, will gain a big fat $6" (Moberg 2003). President Bush is continuing to advocate strongly for additional billions of dollars of tax cuts for wealthier Americans. The justification for the first $1.3 trillion cut was that it would stimulate the economy. Of course, this did not happen; instead, 1.5 million jobs have been lost since January 2001 (Office of Henry Waxman 2002; see also Kelber 2003).

The new justification—since this last one is now laughable—for yet more tax cuts for the rich is floated by one of his spokespersons as follows: "The president is concerned about helping those who are shouldering the burden of this recovery" (Allen and Milbank 2003). In other words, the president has to look after the well-being of the rich since the rich are exploited through taxation. The purpose of this disgraceful public relations spin is to facilitate President Bush's claim that it is the rich who should benefit the most from tax cuts. It is the rich for whom we should feel sorry, according to our president! As observed by economists Heather Boushey and Robert Cherry in an earlier version of their chapter in this volume, Bush, rather than being concerned about poor people and working-class people, has "focused on the 'pain' experienced by those whose stock portfolios have gone south, floating the idea of tax law changes that would allow them to deduct more of their losses from taxable income" (Gale and Orszag 2002 cited in Boushey and Cherry 2002–2003, 52).

The concern regarding the "pain" felt by the rich is associated with the argument that the lopsided concentration of wealth is a rising tide lifting all boats. This is not correct. According to an article by Chuck Collins (1999), "The Wealth Gap Widens," between 1983 and 1995 the net worth of the richest 1 percent grew by 17 percent; but the bottom 40 percent of all households lost 80 percent of net worth as a result of falling wages and rising personal debt. The middle fifth of all households lost 11 percent in spite of earlier tax cuts benefiting the wealthy. As a matter of fact, it is precisely due to the increasing concentration of wealth via tax cuts that ordinary Americans are living in an economic danger zone of increasing personal and consumer debt and bankruptcies. This kind of supply side economics has been a failure for working people, poor families, children, and the elderly, but we know through watching the corruption and greed of entities like Enron that we cannot rely on the self-regulation or altruistic motivations of this sector. Not only does corporate welfare amount to hundreds of billions of dollars yearly that are wasted in terms of economic productivity, but the greed of some corporate leaders has resulted in massive job layoffs, stagnant real wages for working- and middle-class sectors, and the loss of retirement funds and pensions for many elderly Americans.

Within the borders of the most powerful and richest nation in the world, millions of people do not have access to quality health care; millions of children are not only born into poverty, but remain poverty-stricken for most of their lives; millions of families teeter between homelessness and substandard housing; and millions of American families have to meticulously balance work and pocketbooks in order to eat a full meal every day. Sadly, too many Americans have become numb to these kinds of persisting problems and social inequality. They have fallen prey to a modern Horatio Alger mythology about becoming rich that is fueled by lottery tickets and easy access to gambling and casinos. This mythology is encouraged by the politically narcotizing effects of the Hollywood industry with a plethora of shows, soap operas, and ideologically biased news programs that actively dumb down American audiences and keep them blind about injustices.

The call for patriotism under seductive but policy-meaningless phrases like "United We Stand," conjoined with the economic exploitation of working-class people, has been misused by this national administration and corporate wealth to belittle ideals of social justice and concern for human rights and to prevent some Americans from seeing what is in their best social and economic interests. The call for patriotism is misused when the administration calls for "supporting our troops" although many troops return from illegal military adventures without the prospect of full employment, health insurance, or decent and affordable housing for their families. Young people face the prospect of massive layoffs and families have to suffer from cutbacks in critical social services as a result of the economic policies of the national administration. This is glossed over with calls for patriotism and relatively easy access to shiny-looking credit cards with high interest rates.

Related to the overall problem of poverty is the fact that poverty is both racialized and punished as such, though the number and proportion of people of color are growing dramatically. In the United States today, one-half of all black children, and similar proportions of Latino children, and growing numbers of children of Asian descent, and millions of other children remain mired in poverty, or near poverty; millions of these children and their families go without health insurance; and millions of these children go hungry on a daily basis. These kinds of conditions and inequalities have led to an explosion in the prison population, primarily affecting black and Latino youth. Blacks and Latinos make up a significantly higher proportion of prison inmates compared to their proportion of the nation's total population. Prisons housing people of color are growing so fast today that this is actually an industry with a very bright economic future. Many states today spend considerably more on housing inmate populations than on higher education. And in many places our fellow Americans have been reduced to guarding prisoners as their raft or lifeboat in a sea swirling with deteriorating social and economic conditions.

Accompanying these persistent problems is an extraordinary growth in the militarization of U.S. society, both in domestic and foreign spheres. In 2003, the national government approved a $355 billion budget, an increase of $35 billion over 2002. This includes an almost $7 billion antimissile defense similar to Reagan's "Star Wars" fantasy—a program to protect cities and neighborhoods from enemy missiles (Fram 2002). This rapid militarization of U.S. society is a very local matter. The claim that at the local level, in our city councils, in our mayors' offices, in our community-based organizations, we need not focus on growing militarization should be rejected. It is illogical to argue that the military budget is off-limits in discussions about how to turn neighborhoods around. According to a study by the National Priorities Project, Connecticut's share of the proposed missile defense system would be about $156 million, an amount that could be used, instead, to pay for 2,227 affordable housing units or 2,463 new elementary school teachers. The $356 billion, including the increase of $35 billion for 2003 alone, or $1 billion that is spent per day, every day of the year, on the military is a local issue because we pay for it, we subsidize it, and our children and young people will suffer directly the consequences of this madness (National Priorities Project 2002). How can we begin to respond to this kind of situation of racial and ethnic divisions, persistent poverty, growing economic insecurity, and the militarization of our society? To reiterate, I believe that social justice and human rights represent an important foundation for thinking about these issues, a framework far more efficient and effective than simply trying to make the rich richer.

What Is Social Justice?

On a theoretical level, one could use John Rawls and his classic work, *A Theory of Justice*, to answer this question (Rawls 1971). In essence, Rawls argues that everyone should have access to, and enjoy, liberty and income that provide for decent living conditions and that we should not support social or political programs or policies that obstruct, intentionally or unintentionally, the dignity of any human being. Rawls proposes that, at times, inequality is justified but only if it benefits the least among us. Martin Luther King Jr. approached the concept of social justice in a similar way. This position is clear in his use of the biblical parable about the Good Samaritan in his last speech on April 3, 1968, in support of the sanitation workers in Memphis, Tennessee. King's humanistic call for students and leaders to engage in activism against social and economic injustice challenged the assumptions of the dominant civic discourse about race, class, and power. He urged intellectuals and leaders to advance the interests of social democracy for all people, both in the United States and other nations.

In defining social justice I would also make reference to the Universal Declaration of Human Rights adopted by the United Nations on December 10, 1948 (United Nations 1948). This statement represents world opinion and consensus about human rights and social justice that should be integral to any nation. I would point to two articles, in particular, that speak to social justice. The first is Article 23:

> (1) Everyone has the right to work, to free choice of employment, to just and favorable conditions of work and to protection against unemployment. (2) Everyone, without discrimination, has the right to equal pay for equal work. (3) Everyone who works has the right to just and favorable remuneration ensuring for himself and his family an existence worthy of human dignity, and supplemented, if necessary, by other means of social protection. (4) Everyone has the right to form and to join trade unions for the protection of his interests.

And, the second is Article 25:

> (1) Everyone has the right to a standard of living adequate for the health and well-being of himself and of his family, including food, clothing, housing and medical care and necessary social services, and the right to security in the event of unemployment, sickness, disability, widowhood, old age or other lack of livelihood in circumstances beyond his control. (2) Motherhood and childhood are entitled to special care and assistance. All children, whether born in or out of wedlock, shall enjoy the same social protection.

I highlight these articles because they illustrate how current social and economic policies in this country are in violation of both the spirit and substance of this world document.

One public policy that is an example of this violation is welfare reform. This policy represents a radical movement away from the idea of helping children and families and instead seeks to control, monitor, and punish people. It is a policy antithetical to the idea of social justice. So-called welfare reform adopted by the leadership of this nation is in direct violation of Article 25 of the United Nations Declaration of Human Rights because it castigates families and children who are not in a two-parent family; this policy denies people the right and privilege to pursue higher education; it is a policy that discriminates racially and ethnically, and linguistically in the distribution of economic goods.

This policy denies to children and families essential tools for economic survival and self-sufficiency, and degrades people and families who need housing and food. It makes a distinction between deserving children and undeserving children in terms of life necessities and thereby directly violates Article 25 of the Declaration of Human Rights. It is a policy that contributes to worsening local conditions because it ignores the importance of strengthening community-based organizations and small businesses in our neighborhoods.[2] Welfare reform has nothing to do with the reduction of poverty in the midst of vast wealth; this is why it is a human rights issue. Welfare reform perpetuates poverty or near poverty in the midst of increasing and concentrated wealth, making it morally suspect.

Alas, this policy serves a political purpose. So long as we focus on welfare reform in terms of the presumed inadequacies of poor people, we remain blind to corporate welfare. We know through the exposure of corporate officials in companies like Enron and World Com that corporate welfare and corporate waste and greed have destroyed many lives in this country. Yet the dominant civic discourse about our social and economic problems perpetuates a "blame the victim" mentality among the general population that targets people of color and dupes white working-class people into seeing and defining themselves as white, before working-class.

The implication of this statement is that white working-class people in the nation have to redefine themselves as part of a multiracial, multiethnic working class who happen to be white, rather than as part of a "white working class." The organized labor movement has a special responsibility and opportunity in encouraging this change. When the issue of welfare reform was raised, generally speaking, the labor movement did not pay attention, as suggested by Dona Hamilton and Charles V. Hamilton: "In the 1970s the mere suggestion of workfare programs usually brought cries of alarm from unions. . . . During the 1990s the unions have been slow to respond to the workfare program, but as 'downsizing' and layoffs increase, they are beginning to realize that workfare is a menacing threat to their survival" (Hamilton and Hamilton 1997, 264). Although welfare reform threatened worker rights through forced labor and low-wages and represented a divisive wedge among people, labor did not see this attack on poor people as its issue; welfare reform did not seem threatening to white working-class people in the country. Indeed, it was most threatening to the portion of the working class that happens to be white.

The president of TransAfrica, Bill Fletcher, was one of the first labor activists to remind us that welfare reform is an antilabor public policy in terms of its impacts and that welfare recipients are workers (Fletcher 1997). Frances Fox Piven discusses the connections between the politics of public assistance and the idea of "work first" and worker rights in Chapter 1. She describes how welfare reform is fundamentally a mechanism for maintaining class inequality and a weak labor movement. Welfare reform is essentially a policy and program that meets the needs of corporate wealth and globalization to maintain a passive, highly mobile, cheap labor force.

Can We Afford Social Justice in the Midst of Fiscal Distress?

During periods of fiscal stress some might ask: How can we talk of social justice when we have to pay the increasing costs of public services, but have fewer resources or revenues? As reported in the *New York Times*, "Plunging tax collections and soaring medical costs have created the worst fiscal problems for states since World War II" (Pear 2002, 1). Lower tax collections and reductions in federal assistance dollars to states and cities over the last several years mean cuts in employment and training, assisted housing, mass transit, and a range of community development programs. It is this situation that actually supports greater calls for social justice in our public policies. The pursuit of social justice in economic policies is not only cheaper but more effective in creating jobs and a healthy economy than strategies suggested by President Bush and his supporters.

One example of how social justice is more economically efficient in dealing with our problems is provided by Robert B. Reich in his essay, "Whose Tax Cuts?" (Reich 2002). He discusses how much more economically sound it would be to do the right thing by lowering the tax burden of American workers, versus not doing the right thing and repealing the estate tax that primarily benefits rich people. The complete repeal of the estate tax will benefit about 3,000 American families and cost American taxpayers about $700 billion. This is $700 billion that will not be used, necessarily, in any way that will increase the productivity of the U.S. economy. But, if we cared about the working poor, and the working class, we would instead repeal or lower the payroll tax. There are two immediate and favorable results for working-class people with this approach. First, workers would have more money to spend and thereby fuel additional economic activity. But, second, there would be lessening of the burden on small businesses, which would then keep employed more workers and families.

Another example is shared by Lawrence Mishel, president of the Economic Policy Institute in Washington, D.C. (Mishel 2002). Mishel's argument is that expenditures on education, school repairs and renovation, extending unemployment benefits, and other social goods represent an economic stimulus plan that would make the most sense not just in creating jobs, but also in strengthening the economy. The kind of economic stimulus package described here would also reduce the effects of income and wealth inequality in the nation. Doing the right thing with these kinds of initiatives would have an immediate economic benefit for millions of Americans. Both these examples show that social justice does not contradict good economic sense.

Can We Pursue Both Social Justice and a "War Against Terrorism"?

The idea of social justice might be disparaged as utopian, inefficient, or even inappropriate at this time due to the nation's "war against terrorism." The call for social justice, or the expansion of labor rights, or the strengthening of our civil rights, or respecting the human rights of people in other nations, could even be considered unpatriotic today. Catchy and seductive phrases like the "war against terrorism," "homeland security," "regime change," and the dubiously titled U.S. Patriot Act make it possible to consider calls for social justice as suspect. Already, people who advocate social justice and civil protections have been painted by some government officials and political leaders as naive or "unpatriotic." Note the chilling warning of the attorney general for the United States of America, John Ashcroft, during a U.S. Senate hearing: "To those who scare peace-loving people with phantoms of lost liberty, my message is this: Your tactics only aid terrorists, for they erode our national unity and diminish our resolve. They give ammunition to America's enemies and pause to America's friends" (Ashcroft 2001). Given the strong link between social justice and civil rights in this country, and personal liberties for all people, remarks like these will make it a bit easier to accuse those who promote social justice of being unpatriotic.

The ideological, journalistic, or political lynching of those who call for change on behalf of social justice is also not new in this country. In the 1950s, when Americans stood up for social justice, when they demanded the end of apartheid in this country, when they called for the expansion of health care, quality education, and affordable, decent housing for fellow citizens who were impoverished, and when they dared to suggest that perhaps the United States should desist from foreign policies and practices that disrespected the self-determination of other nations, such as "regime change" and the assassination of political leaders, these Americans were called, "un-American" or unpatriotic. And many were investigated by the House Un-American Activities Committee under U.S. Senator Joseph McCarthy.

When Martin Luther King Jr. emerged as an eloquent and effective spokesperson for a national vision and politics based on social justice, what was said about him? Even some national leaders supporting civil rights belittled him for mixing these two kinds of issues. King's vision of social justice led him to advocate the elimination of poverty in the midst of plenty. He called for social policies like universal health insurance so that people would not have to suffer physical, or mental, or emotional illnesses simply because they could not afford basic health care. His call for social justice and respect for human rights was treated as un-patriotic and seditious by many people and leaders. Contemporary terminology focused on homeland security similarly belittles or neutralizes concern for social justice.

These undefined and loaded terms cannot provide comprehensive answers to the economic challenges facing U.S. society. A notion of social justice can be comprehensive, facilitating the transformation of problems into opportunities for all people. How would strategies and programs reflecting calls for social justice look today? First, our public policies regarding social problems would be preventive and comprehensive, rather than reactive or punitive. For example, we would not have a "war against drugs"; drug addiction would be approached as a public health issue, not a crime. Public policy would indeed reflect a strong family orientation in that supportive services would be available to bolster the economic security of all families regardless of their composition or religion; we would not discriminate against families whether they are headed by women or men, or by single or married adults. We would presume that all families raising children require a basic economic floor and access to health and housing. Certainly health care would be available for all people regardless of their economic situation; no one would be denied basic health care due to their particular economic status, as is the practice in most of the world today. And education would be based on the presumption that every child is a potential genius in some area of activity; there would be a focus on ensuring that public schools enjoy the same kind of resources, including dedicated teachers and educators, that are found in private schools, rather than the focus on high-stakes testing that only ensures that many children will be left behind. These are the kinds of national policies that could immediately help cities and neighborhoods and serve to bring people together.

Unfortunately, the *New York Times* article by Paul Zielbauer cited earlier did not provide an adequate answer to its own query regarding how to save the city of Hartford. In essence, the article argues for bringing back a middle class as salvation for this city. The article focused on huge megaprojects, including a convention center and giant hotel costing almost $800 billion that hopefully can "attract suburban empty-nesters" and make the city a "weekend destination for families across Southern New England." Actually, this is the same blueprint suggested by others as a way of saving cities and neighborhoods. Two writers, Dennis R. Judd and Todd Swanstrom, describe and critique this kind of blueprint as the "logic of growth politics."[3] As suggested earlier, this refers to support for huge projects and economic policies (including reductions in the taxation burdens for corporations and the rich) that are aimed at subsidizing corporate wealth in the hope that it will mean economic opportunities for poor people and working-class people and their neighborhoods. I would propose, again, that pursuing social justice as a value in our society points the way to more creative approaches for revitalizing our cities and neighborhoods. The latter focuses on enhancing the quality of civic participation in these places and strengthening the institutional infrastructure that serves people. It calls for resources that increase the capacity of small businesses serving residents; it seeks to strengthen linkages between different racial and ethnic groups of people and between generations; it is based on the pursuit and creation of living-wage jobs for Americans. These goals and related strategies are not part of our current national dialogues. This is unfortunate because until we seek to do the right thing by helping all people and expanding our social and economic democracy, we will not be doing the right thing for our collective future.

Notes

1. See the following two related works for overviews and analysis of racial and economic problems facing U.S. society today: Stokes, Martinez, and Rhodes-Reed (2001) and Stokes and Melendez (2003).

2. Ken Neubeck and Noel Cazenave show in their book, *Welfare Racism* (2001), that this is not an ad hoc type of discrimination; it is not accidental or unintentional discrimination. Rather, the racial, ethnic, and linguistic discrimination that is associated with the implementation of welfare reform is functional and systematic in supporting economic policies favoring the rich in U.S. society.

3. See Judd and Swanstrom (1994), especially Chapter 13, titled "Urban Economic Development: Who Wins and Who Loses?"

References

Allen, Mike, and Donna Milbank. 2003. "President to Seek Dividend Tax Cut." *Washington Post*, 3 January, A1.

Ashcroft, John. 2001. "Testimony of Attorney General John Ashcroft to the Senate Committee on the Judiciary." 6 December. Available at www.usdoj.gov/ag/testimony/2001/1206transcriptsenatejudiciarycommittee.htm.

Boushey, Heather, and Robert Cherry. 2002/03. "The Severe Implications of the Economic Downturn on Working Families." *Working USA* 6, no. 3 (winter): 35–54.

Collins, Chuck. 1999. "The Wealth Gap Widens." *Dollars and Sense*, no. 225 (September/October): 12–13.

DuBois, W.E.B. 1970. "The Revelation of Saint Orgne the Damned." In *W.E.B. Speaks: Speeches and Addresses*, ed. Philip S. Foner. New York: Pathfinder Press.

Fletcher, Bill. 1997. "Seizing the Time Because the Time Is Now: Welfare Repeal and Labor Reconstruction." In *Audacious Democracy: Labor, Intellectuals, and the Social Reconstruction of America*, ed. Steven Fraser and Joshua B. Freeman. Boston: Houghton Mifflin.

Fram, Alan. 2002. "Senate OKs $355 Billion for Defense." *Bergen County Record*, 2 August, A11.

Gale, William, and Peter Orszag. 2002. "A New Round of Tax Cuts?" Brookings Institution, working paper, 22 August.

Hamilton, Dona Cooper, and Charles V. Hamilton. 1997. *Dual Agenda: Race and Social Welfare Policies of the Civil Rights Organization*. New York: Columbia University Press.

Jennings, James. 1994. *Understanding the Nature of Poverty*. Westport, CT: Praeger.

Judd, Dennis R., and Todd Swanstrom. 1994. *City Politics: Private Power and Public Policy*. New York: Harper Collins.

Kelber, Harry. 2003. "Will Bush's Huge Tax Cuts for Investors Create Jobs for Unemployed Americans?" *Labor Talk*, 8 January. Available at www.laboreducator.org/ctcrjb/htm.

Mishel, Lawrence. 2002. "Generating Jobs and Growth: An Economic Stimulus Plan for 2003." Briefing paper. Washington, DC: Economic Policy Institute.

Moberg, David. 2003. "The Real Class War." In *These Times* 27, no. 6 (February): 20–22.

National Priorities Project. 2002. "Military Spending and What It Could Really Pay For." Northampton, MA: National Priorities Project. Available at www.nationalpriorities.org/issues/military/tradeoffs.html.

Neubeck, Kenneth, and Noel Cazenave. 2001. *Welfare Racism: Playing the Race Card Against America's Poor*. New York: Routledge Press.

Palley, Thomas I. 2000. *Plenty of Nothing: The Downsizing of the American Dream and the Case for Structural Keynesianism*. Princeton, NJ: Princeton University Press.

Pear, Robert. 2002. "States Are Facing Big Fiscal Crisis, Governors Report." *New York Times*, 26 November, A1.

Rawls, John. 1971. *A Theory of Justice*. Cambridge, MA: Harvard University Press.

Reich, Robert B. 2002. "Whose Tax Cuts?" *The American Prospect* 13, no. 22 (December): 2–3.

Stokes, Curtis, Theresa Martinez, and Genice Rhodes-Reed. 2001. *Race in 21st Century America*. East Lansing: Michigan State University Press.

Stokes, Curtis, and Theresa Melendez. 2003. *Racial Liberalism and the Politics of Urban America*. East Lansing: Michigan State University Press.

United Nations. 1948. "Universal Declaration of Human Rights." General Assembly Resolution 217 A (III). Available at www.un.org/Overview/rights.html.

Waxman, Office of Henry. 2002. "Are You Better Off Today Than You Were Two Years Ago?" Fact sheet. September 30.

Zielbauer, Paul. 2002. "Poverty in a Land of Plenty: Can Hartford Ever Recover?" *New York Times*, 26 August, A1.

About the Editor and Contributors

Fran Bernstein is a policy analyst with the American Federation of State, County and Municipal Employees' (AFSCME) Legislation Department. She is responsible for analyzing federal policies in the areas of social services and health care.

Heather Boushey is with the Center for Economic and Policy Research. Her primary areas of research are the U.S. labor market, social policy, and work and family issues. She is coauthor of *The State of Working America, 2002–03* and she has testified before Congress, and written numerous reports and commentaries on the effectiveness of the 1996 welfare reform.

Robert Cherry is an economics professor at Brooklyn College of City University of New York. His most recent book is *Who Gets the Good Jobs? Combatting Race and Gender Disparities*, and he continues to work with Max Sawicky at the Economic Policy Institute on a proposal to universalize the earned income tax credit.

James Jennings is professor of urban and environmental policy and planning at Tufts University. He has published numerous books and articles on race and urban politics and on public policy. His books include *Welfare Reform and the Revitalization of Inner City Communities* (2003), *Race and Politics* (1998), and *Blacks, Latinos, and Asians: Status and Prospects for Activism* (1996).

Chirag Mehta is a research associate with the University of Illinois at Chicago Center for Urban Economic Development. His area of research includes low-wage labor market analysis, labor market policy interventions, and welfare reform policy.

Immanuel Ness researches organizing of low-wage workers, immigrants, and people of color and is completing a book on immigrant self-organization in New York. He is associate professor in political science at Brooklyn College, City University of New York. He also is editor of *Working USA* and the author, with Stuart Eimer, of *Central Labor Councils and the Revival of American Unionism* (2001).

David J. Olson is a professor in the Political Science Department at the University of Washington, where he founded and formerly directed the Center for Labor Studies. He has published several books and numerous articles on national, state, and urban politics in the United States, and his current research focuses on labor-related issues.

Cecilia Perry is a public policy analyst with AFSCME's Research Department. She is responsible for analyzing policies from state and local perspectives in the areas of cash assistance, food stamps, child care, Head Start, and child welfare.

Frances Fox Piven is an internationally known author and activist whose work in social theory and political sociology has focused on the role of social movements in democratic social change. She is the author of numerous prize-winning books, and her work reflects her preoccupation with the uses of social science to promote social reform. She is Distinguished Professor in Political Science and Sociology at the Graduate Center of City University of New York.

Max B. Sawicky is an economist at the Economic Policy Institute. He has worked in the Office of State and Local Finance of the U.S. Treasury Department and the U.S. Advisory Commission on Intergovernmental Relations. He also serves on the at-large national board of Americans for Democratic Action.

Louise Simmons is associate professor of social work and director of the Urban Semester Program at the University of Connecticut. She is involved in several community-labor coalitions in Connecticut and her work focuses on urban politics, progressive urban social movements, community-labor coalitions, and welfare policy. She wrote *Organizing in Hard Times: Labor and Neighborhoods in Hartford* (1994) and served on the Hartford City Council in the early 1990s.

Erich Steinman is a doctoral student in sociology at the University of Washington. His master's thesis examined variation in the male-female wage gap across occupations, and his dissertation addresses the emergence of American Indian tribes as sovereign governments in the contemporary policy era.

Nik Theodore is an assistant professor in the Urban Planning and Policy Program and research director of the Center for Urban Economic Development at the University of Illinois at Chicago.

Helena Worthen is assistant professor of labor education in the Labor Education Program at the University of Illinois at Chicago. Her previous work on occupational and technical programs in community colleges is found in W.N. Grubb and Associates, *Honored but Invisible: An Inside Look at Teaching in Community Colleges* (1999).

Roland Zullo researches unions, politics, and privatization within the U.S. system. He is a research scientist with the University of Michigan Institute of Labor and Industrial Relations.

Index